4/22/19

To: My c

May you c _____ th
grace & the knowledge of God
who is more than able to do all
that He has promised to do in
and through you. May this book
Provide some encouragement for
you journey.

Love,
Cuz Jen

Happy Birthday.. May God
continues to bless you richly.

That I May Know You

Terry Michaels

Strategic Book Publishing
New York, New York

All Scripture quotations are taken from the King James Version of the Bible.

Strategic Book Publishing
An imprint of AEG Publishing Group
845 Third Avenue, 6th Floor – 6016
New York, NY 10022
http://www.strategicbookpublishing.com

ISBN: 978-1-60693-487-6, 1-60693-487-2

Book Design: Bruce Salender

Printed in the United States of America.

Dedicated to
'Tilly'
My amazing new grandbaby
That she would know God.

Table of Contents

Table of Contents

Acknowledgements

First and foremost I give thanks to God for granting me the ability to put my thoughts on paper. The inspiration for this book comes directly from His Word.

Props to my daughter, Carly Skelton, for cleaning up the original draft of this manuscript.

Kudos to my editors Stephanie Nickel and Al Boyce. Many thanks to all the fine people at Strategic Book Publishers.

I can't forget my wife, Christy, who encouraged me in this writing.

To all my brothers and sisters at Calvary Chapel of the Springs, thank you for your friendship, prayers and support.

Preface

What if? What if we really took the daddy of all commandments seriously? No doubt, you know the one I'm talking about. Jesus called it the first and the greatest. He charged, *"Thou shalt love the Lord thy God with all thy heart, and with all thy soul, and with all thy mind"* (Matthew 22:37). This is where all fall short. We also fall short of excuses. How does one justify not loving the Lord enough? We can't fault heredity or society can we? We can't point the finger at others. Heck, we can't even excuse it as some genetic flub – *"Sorry, Lord, I'm devotionally challenged!"* No, we have only ourselves to blame. Love is something we willfully choose whether or not to do. When it comes to loving God with the entirety of our heart, mind and soul - every one of us misses the mark. True, some love God more than others, but even they'd tell you they don't love Him nearly enough.

Think about it, do you love God with all that is within you? Have you committed your entire being to loving Him? Are you completely obsessed with loving Him each and every day, every moment of the day? Excuse me for relying on rhetoric from the disco era, but I ask the very question asked by the Bee Gees, "How deep is your love?" Let's face it; we all have room for growth in this area. And that's the exciting thing about being a child of God. We get to watch love grow! We can grow closer to the Lord and as we do, we fall more deeply in love with Him. That is what the Christian experience is all about. If you thought it was about religion or rituals or signing off on a long list of rules and regulations, you are sorely mistaken. Christianity is more of an adventure, a divine romance, in which we pursue God and seek to know Him more. It's about spending time in His presence, experiencing the love He gives and channeling that love right back where it came from. This is where I intend to take you. I hope this writing encourages you in your relationship with the Lord. I hope you can say by the end of each chapter, "I know God a little better." By the time you finish this book, I hope you'll be able to say, "I love God a whole lot more!" Is this your desire? Well then, read on!

A Word Before

Before venturing into the first section of this book, you may want to read Exodus chapters 32 and 33. This is where we find the nation of Israel feeling stranded in the wilderness. Acting upon their frustrations, the unhappy wanderers soon turn their backs on the Lord and manufacture a new god; one reflective of their carnal nature. While this proves to be a low point in the history of Israel, it becomes an exceptionally high point in the life of their leader. He seeks hard after the true and living God. This book follows upon this one man's heels. From his example, we learn what it means to have a passion for God and how we can experience the power of His presence in our lives. Before reading any further, I'd like to share with you the prayer which serves as the inspiration for this writing. Though I cannot take credit for this little gem, I have made it my own. May this brief yet powerful prayer be yours as well!

"Now therefore, I pray thee, if I have found grace in thy sight, show me now thy way, that I may know thee, that I may find grace in thy sight: and consider that this nation is thy people" (Exodus 33:13).

Section I
Promise

"Blessed be the LORD, that hath given rest unto his people Israel, according to all that he promised: there hath not failed one word of all his good promise, which he promised by the hand of Moses his servant" (1 Kings 8:56).

Promise: [Hebrew, dabar] word

I've never been to a *Promise Keepers'* gathering -- only because I'm not sure that I am one. I'd like to say that I was, but my track record does not reflect absolute perfection in this area. Of the thousands of men who have attended *Promise Keepers* rallies, I wonder how many have actually remained true to their commitment to be better husbands and fathers. We'd have to ask their wives and children to get a real answer, but I'd venture to say the statistics might be disappointing. I do know of one man who is actively involved with *Promise Keepers*. He left his first wife to be with his second. He then left his second to be with his third. He abandoned his third within one year's time. It seems odd to me that someone so unfaithful in marriage could actively be so involved in a group called *"Promise Keepers."* It is not my intention to bash this well-meaning organization or what it stands for. The only point I wish to make here is that people aren't perfect. Therefore, odds don't stack in our favor when it comes to keeping our word. The history of man, even as far back as Adam, attests to the fact that we are not promise keepers at all. Our past is checkered with promises made and promises broken. It has been said that the best predictor of future behavior is past behavior. This pearl of wisdom alerts us to a proven pattern when it comes to the human race. Time has not made us more trustworthy. In the Bible we meet only one promise keeper – God! His track record is perfect. He has never broken His Word, not even once! If the best predictor of future behavior is indeed past behavior, there should be no difficulty at all with trusting Him.

The promise highlighted in the above caption [1 Kings 8:56] is one of rest. I tend to associate rest with naptime. This is why I have difficulty referring to the bathroom as a restroom. It's not a place I'd ever want to pull out a cot. But this is not the type of rest God speaks of. He's talking about relief. The Lord kept His Word by relieving His people from slavery in Egypt. Furthermore, He promised them a future and a hope in a land flowing with milk and honey. The appropriate response to God's promises is praise. Sadly, the Israelites didn't see it that way. They murmured and whined. This was the beginning of their decline. Before long they strayed from the Lord, then sought to replace Him *(which they promised never to do).* This is the sad digression we see with God's people in the Exodus story: it begins with dissatisfaction, which turns to distance, and then to all-out disobedience. Yet in a sea of wayward wanderers we find one courageous enough to seek the God of rest. This is his story. His name is Moses.

Chapter 1
Milk and Honey

"... I will bring you up out of the affliction of Egypt unto the land of the Canaanites, and the Hittites, and the Amorites, and the Perizzites, and the Hivites, and the Jebusites, unto a land flowing with milk and honey" (Exodus 3:17).

The Lord not only promised to relieve His people of their agony, He vowed to bless them abundantly. Israel would be rescued from captivity and returned to the 'land of plenty' once again. Their deliverance would be immediate. The promise of abundance would be realized a little later, after some wandering in the wilderness. Yet even in the wilderness the Israelites tasted of God's glory and experienced the richness of His grace beyond measure. Each family left Egypt with a handful of loot, which was a most miraculous provision only the Lord can be credited for.[1]

---

[1] Exodus 12:35-36

Then there was the quail, the manna from heaven and water from a rock, all supernaturally provided from above. The glory of God came in the form of a pillar of cloud by day and a pillar of fire by night. All these served to affirm Israel that the Lord was faithful and that His word could be counted upon.

What holds true for Israel holds true for the children of God today. Our deliverance comes immediate. The moment we call upon Him, He frees us from the shackles of sin. Furthermore, God vows to get us to that place of promise, that heavenly city where His generosity is cranked on overflow. Jesus assures us, *"And if I go and prepare a place for you, I will come again, and receive you unto myself; that where I am, there ye may be also."* (John 14:3) In the meantime, we are wanderers. This world is not our home, it's our wilderness. We're just passing through. Even still, we've got our paws on a handful of loot! The Apostle Paul declared, *"Blessed be the God and Father of our Lord Jesus Christ, who hath blessed us with all spiritual blessings in heavenly places in Christ"* (Ephesians 1:3). Yes, even in our wilderness we can taste Heaven and capture wonderful glimpses of God's glory. We can experience His love, forgiveness, grace, joy and, yes, His rest! And rather than a pillar of cloud or fire leading from afar, we have God's own Spirit leading from within. James nailed it when he wrote, *"Every good gift and every perfect gift is from above, and cometh down from the Father of lights, with whom is no variableness, neither shadow of turning"* (James 1:17). What gets us into trouble is when we lose sight of these heavenly perks. How happy we are when we are mindful of them!

Compared to where we will one day be, we are only sipping water from a rock and nibbling on manna crumbs. Both represent Jesus, by the way (see 1 Corinthians 10:4 and John 6:31-33). One day we will be swimming in milk and honey! One might ask, "What's so appealing about milk and honey?" Obviously, it held great promise for the

Israelites, and not because they were tea lovers. Let's think this through. First we'll serve up the "leche." To have a land flowing with milk, you need cattle by the gazillions. Next, you need pastureland and acres upon acres. This all requires fertile soil, sunshine, rain, etc. Then there's the honey. For a land to be dripping in it you need lots of bees, pollination, flowers, plants, trees, soil, more sunshine, more rain and the list goes on. (Leave it to the cute little bees and cattle to keep everything well pollinated and fertilized.) I'm sure you get the picture by now. A land flowing with milk and honey speaks of abundance! It promises a future and hope, prosperity and security, luxury and livelihood. We can even look ahead in the *Book of Isaiah* and see how God's people arrived in the Promised Land with silver spoons in each of their mouths:

> *"Now will I sing to my well-beloved a song of my beloved touching his vineyard. My well-beloved hath a vineyard in a very fruitful hill: And he fenced it, and gathered out the stones thereof, and planted it with the choicest vine, and built a tower in the midst of it, and also made a winepress therein: and he looked that it should bring forth grapes, and it brought forth wild grapes"* (Isaiah 5:1-2).

Sadly, the above love song ends on a sour note. We see a vineyard with incredible potential producing nothing but bitter fruit. In this poignant ode, Isaiah's beloved is the Lord. The vineyard represents Israel, the very people we find wandering in the wilderness with Moses. Though it would take an entire generation for God's people to return to the land of promise, we see from Isaiah's song that the conditions were absolutely ideal for a fresh, new start. Firstly, the vineyard was situated on a fruitful hill. Vine-yards are often planted on slopes to allow for proper drain-age. This way plants don't die from root rot. Hills also allow for steady run-off so crops below can be irrigated. This tells us that Israel was positioned to bless others. She was to be a land *flowing* with milk and honey not *flooded* with milk and honey. Where I live, in the Texas Hill Country, we get a good measure of rain. We appreciate wet weather as it keeps things green, lush and beautiful. From time to time, it may also flood in our area. The results are devastating. God poured into Israel that she might pour out to others. She was to be flowing -- not flooded. Unfortunately, Israel soaked up her blessings but became a lousy dispenser. Her people eventually got 'run off' because there was no healthy runoff. As Christians, we are never to grow soggy either. Living water must pour out as quickly as it pours in. Should we horde, our roots will rot and we will wither.

We also learn from Isaiah's song that God placed great value on Israel. While some at this point may think of ancient Israel as a worthless stick in the mud, our loving Father refers to it as the '*choicest*' vine. The choicest vines are the reddest ones. They yield luscious purple grapes which are used for fine wines. Finally, God placed a winepress in His vineyard. This shows us that God anticipated a lot of _good_ fruit. The best way to tell a good grape from a bad one is to crush it. That's what the winepress is, it's a crusher. Its purpose is to produce something better, not bitter. When you crush good grapes, the flesh is torn away and out pours sweet wine. Wild grapes just *whine* when crushed. God does allow his children to go through the crusher. He uses this process to tear away at our flesh, build character and produce spiritual depth. If we're not growing better it's because we're bitter.

God uses the wilderness as a winepress. What robbed Israel of her blessings was bitterness. This thankless bunch continued to bellyache. Rather than praise, they chose to protest; instead of rejoicing, they revolted. Good fruit can never be produced under these conditions, there will only be sour grapes. Only by embracing the presence of God can one become fruitful. Jesus said, *"Without me ye can do nothing."[1]* Unless we're abiding, we're backsliding. One obvious symptom of backsliding is an ungrateful heart. We lose sight of what God has done, what He is doing and what He has promised to do. That's when we wither up like a dry branch. Thus, we cease to produce any good fruit. This was the condition of Israel while in the wilderness. These were the kinds of people Moses had to put up with for four grueling decades. They lost sight of the promise and ultimately dove headlong into sin.

---

[1] John 15:5

Section II
Sin

"For all have sinned, and come short of the glory of God."
(Romans 3:23).

"For the wages of sin is death" (Romans 6:23a).

Sin: [Greek, hamartano] to miss the mark.

Even at age 10 my brother, Rick, was dangerously overconfident in himself. Most thought he was joking when he had 4-year-old Jimmy Burnet stand against the garage door so he could shoot an arrow over his head. Jimmy co-operated while the rest of us kids anxiously watched on. No one believed Rick would actually follow through with such a foolish dare. To our surprise, he pulled back on his bow, focused carefully on his target and then let the arrow rip from his puny fingers. Within seconds a small spear stuck out of the garage door only a fraction of an inch above Jimmy's spinning head. The bewildered boy turned a whiter shade of pale after seeing the close call on his young life. Had my brother missed the mark, even by a fraction, the result could have been fatal.

The word used for sin in our Bible comes from an archery term meaning "to miss the mark." If you happen to play darts, your mark is that little red dot in the center of the target. If you have ever missed the bull's eye, even just once, guess what? You're guilty of sin! This is why religion cannot save anyone. Even in our feeble attempts to do good we miss the mark. With all the various Christian denominations we have today, it is easy to conclude that no one is truly on target. Man's aim is not steady enough to reverse the curse of death; we only add sin upon sin if we think so. We have but one hope – God! Only He can save us from our wretched condition. Sadly, the Israelites looked elsewhere.

Chapter 2
Holy Cow!

Lessons from Exodus 32

"And the LORD said unto Moses, Go, get thee down; for thy people, which thou broughtest out of the land of Egypt, have corrupted themselves: They have turned aside quickly out of the way which I commanded them: they have made them a molten calf, and have worshiped it, and have sacrificed thereunto, and said, These be thy gods, O Israel, which have brought thee up out of the land of Egypt" (Exodus 32:7-8).

In the case of Israel, absence did not make the heart grow fonder. Quite the opposite, the hearts of these antsy wanderers grew restless. As far as they could see, their leader was dilly-dallying on the mountaintop way too long. It did not seem fair that everyone else had to wait it out while Moses and God took their sweet time getting all clingy with each other. After a long stretch of 40 days it was finally suggested to Pastor Aaron, *"It's time we do a little creating of our own! Let's make another god who will lead us!"* What they really wanted was a god they could lead by the nostrils and one that wouldn't mind all their relentless bellyaching! Aaron was agreeable to the idea and quickly championed an idol fund, collecting ear and nose jewelry from the entire congregation. Once the donations were received, Aaron went right to work. The gold was melted and molded and before long Rev. Aaron was introducing the Mighty Moo saying, *"Israel, here are your gods who brought you out of Egypt."* Not only did Aaron introduce the golden calf as the god of Israel, he built an altar before it and declared a national holiday in its honor. When Moses saw the golden calf, he practically had a cow himself. His own brother (and second-hand-man) had given Israel a bum-steer! So incensed was Moses, he smashed the stone tablets which God Himself had etched His Word upon.

As is generally the case, idolatry quickly led to immorality. Members of the Mighty Moo movement celebrated their holiday by dropping trou'. The Exodus story tells us, *"And they rose up early on the morrow, and offered burnt offerings, and brought peace offerings; and the people sat down to eat and to drink, and rose up to play"* (32:6). Some Bible translations say 'orgy' rather than 'play'. What's clear is that these moo-nies were engaged in a lot more than just an innocent game of *pin the tail on the calf.* It was a full-on sex party! Bear in mind that these idolatrous party animals were believers. They had seen God's presence descend upon the mountaintop and they had heard the thunder of His voice as He spoke with Moses. Also, the Red Sea had been parted right before their eyes. Then there was the pillar of cloud by day and the pillar of fire by night. These people had all kinds of experiences with God. As wonderful as each of these happenings were, faith cannot survive on supernatural experiences alone. Without a personal relationship with God, faith is flakey at best. As for the Israelites, they did not deny God. They simply preferred another one, one who would serve their carnal desires. And sadly, the only time we find these people enthusiastic about anything in the Exodus story is when they are worshipping a metallic beast.

Just to give you an idea of how fickle the Israelites had become, let's look at the agreement they had entered into with their God. The Lord had declared to His people, *"Now therefore, if ye will obey my voice indeed, and keep my covenant, then ye shall be a peculiar treasure unto me above all people: for all the earth is mine"* (Exodus 19:5). With one voice they vowed, *"All that the LORD hath spoken we will do"* (Exodus 19:8). Cooperative, aren't they? Now let's look at what the Lord instructed them as quoted from Exodus 20:23, *"Ye shall not make with me gods of silver, neither shall ye make unto you gods of gold."* Forty days later and what are they doing? They're carving cow! How did it happen? It began when they lost their appreciation for God. They lost sight of what God had done: delivering them from slavery, parting the Red Sea, providing quail, manna and water from a rock. They lost sight of what God was doing. He was imparting His Word to Moses, words designed to protect and preserve Israel as the Lord's own special possession. They lost sight of what God promised to do: prosper them in a land flowing with milk and honey.

Once our appreciation for the Lord goes out the window, we are no longer bowing to Him. If we won't bow to Him, we will bow to something else -- something reflective of our own carnal nature. That's why idolatry always leads to immorality. It's a celebration of self and all that the flesh craves. It may look like a cow or another creature, but it's actually the inner beast that replaces God. What we see here is three tell-tale signs of a backslidden condition:

thanklessness, self-absorption and, finally, immorality. We can only overcome through an upward focus on God. We must always be mindful of what God has done, is doing and has promised to do.

Chapter 3
God Gets No Credit

*"And he received them at their hand, and fash-
ioned it with a graving tool, after he had made
it a molten calf: and they said, These be thy
gods, O Israel, which brought thee up out of the
land of Egypt"* (Exodus 32:4)

Aaron's golden calf served the same purpose as Nim-
rod's *Tower of Babel*. Both were attempts to canonize
mankind without having to play by God's rules. There
wasn't any requirement for faith or relationship or righteousness. All one needed was a little bit of religion and a
belief in the existence of a higher power. You see, God
wasn't completely swept under the carpet when calf worship was introduced. As a matter of fact, Israel's Holy Cow
Day was to be a festival in the Lord's honor.[1] And just how
did they honor the Lord? Immediately prior to their little

---

[1] Exodus 32:5

sex party, they brought sacrificial offerings to the golden calf. In essence, the Israelites had made idol worship synonymous with Jehovah worship. Calling this Holy Cow day a "festival in the Lord's honor" was perhaps Aaron's biggest blunder of all. In so doing, he dishonored the name of God and reduced Him to an impotent creature -- not even a real creature but an artificial one!

Early manuscripts of the Old Testament tell us that Aaron literally referred to this crude cow carnival as, "a festival in *YHWH's* honor." In ancient times God's name was so revered scribes dared not even spell it out. Even today the pronunciation of YHWH remains somewhat of a mystery. Some have played *Wheel of Fortune* with the name of God and bought a couple of vowels to help us articulate it. The most common of these names would be Yahweh or Jehovah, but even these are mere educated guesses. In the Hebrew, however, there does seem to be a close connection between YHWH and I AM, the name God used when introducing Himself to Moses in the burning bush. Though we are uncertain as to how this name is to be pronounced, we do know that God's name is holy, it is not to be taken in vain and it is never to be pinned onto a calf or any other creature.

It is likely that Aaron's inspiration for the golden calf came straight from Egypt where there were scores of these four-legged images. The sacred cow of the Egyptians was "Apis." It represented fertility and "the renewal of life." To quote from the on-line encyclopedia Wikipedia, *"Apis was the most important of all the sacred animals in Egypt, and, like the others, its importance increased as time went on."* Wikipedia goes on to say, *"The Apis bull was considered to be a manifestation of the pharaoh."* Keep in mind that the pharaohs of antiquity were all regarded as deity. This is who the Egyptians looked to for their milk and honey. Were the Israelites also looking to a deified cow for their milk and honey? Most likely they were. We can conclude that they trusted the calf for what God promised to do because they had already given the calf credit for what God had already done. It was declared, *"These be thy gods, O Israel, which brought thee up out of the land of Egypt."*

The most abominable thing about idol worship is that God is not given the credit He deserves -- the creature gets all the glory. When I was small, I wore an image of St. Christopher around my neck, thinking he would protect me. He was the one I trusted to keep me from harm's way. And he got the credit for my safety. Where do we get these wild ideas? They come from the imagination of man. Even though it may be filtered through a church or a "holy man" who believes in the existence of the Almighty, the idea of saint patrol does not jive with God's Word. The Bible tells us that the Lord is our deliverer, not some deceased do-gooder. Scripture also assures that there is no interaction between the saints above and the saints below.[1]

Most who are led down this sorrowful path don't know better. They would never think of themselves as idolaters, but consider themselves in good Christian company. Their "Christian" upbringing has taught them to trust in created beings rather than the Creator. This is because their religious affiliation has incorporated idol worship with Jehovah worship. I speak from personal experience when I say that many of these idolaters are sincere people who truly believe they are honoring God. But, sadly, they've been given a bum steer. There are some who chant endless prayers to Mary in wake of a loved one's death. This tradition is practiced because it is believed that the deceased's stay in purgatory will be shortened through Mary's intervention. It is taught in their catechism that she too ascended unto heaven without sin. This makes her uniquely qualified to intercede for others. No wonder there are countless shrines in her honor throughout the globe! While Mary is to

---

[1] Luke 16:20-31

be appreciated for her role in the life of Jesus, she is not worthy of the credit which is due unto God alone. It is through His atoning work that we are saved from sin and nothing else. Mary, like you and I, is a created being. God is not honored when man bows before her image or any other. Whether it would be a cow or your favorite Bible character, save Jesus, this is idolatry. It is an abomination to the Lord.

Even Ol' Saint Pete, as esteemed as he is and as proud as he was, would not allow himself to be idolized. Upon entering the home of Captain Cornelius, this awestruck Italian officer bowed before Peter and worshipped him. But... *"Peter took him up, saying, Stand up; I myself also am a man."* (Acts 10:26) God's Word goes on to forbid the worship of angels. In the book of Revelation we find the Apostle John encountering one of these heavenly creatures. John writes, *"And I fell at his feet to worship him. And he said unto me, 'See thou do it not: I am thy fellow servant, and of thy brethren that have the testimony of Jesus: worship God!'"* (Revelation 19:10) There is only one who is worthy of our worship. It is God alone. Many try to play semantic games with God's Word to get around this. They say, "Well, it's not really worship, it's just 'adoration' or 'appreciation.'" Listen, if you are bowing to the creature, praying to the creature, lighting candles to the creature or erecting images of the creature, scripture has no other name for it than idolatry. God also assures us in His word that idolatry makes Him jealous.

Even Aaron knew deep within his heart that what he did was abominable. But he wasn't about to assume any personal responsibility for his actions. He quickly pointed the finger at everyone else. When Moses demanded an explanation, Aaron quickly passed the buck whimpering, *"Let not the anger of my lord wax hot: thou knowest the people, that they are set on mischief."*[1] Say, didn't Adam try that one when God called him on the carpet? In his case, there was only one other person he could possibly blame; the fact that it was his wife didn't deter him one iota. *"The woman whom You gave to be with me,"* Adam declared, *"she gave me of the tree, and I ate."*[2] Every sin known to man rides on the back of some scapegoat and comes neatly wrapped with excuses. Somehow we think we can crawl out of that wrapper as if we were never part of it. Aaron sure tried.

To add insult to injury, Aaron claimed that the cow just happened to pop out of the fire after throwing in a wad of *bling-bling.* This is another clever technique man uses to justify wrongdoing. It's the old "it all happened quite innocently" song and dance. Rev. Aaron put on his dancing shoes then told his brother to lighten up. Moses did not lighten up, though. He didn't buy into Aaron's sorry excuses. He called it like it was. Moses did not say, "Oh well, everybody makes mistakes." On the contrary he said, *"Ye have sinned a great sin."* Israel's offense was a gross one. They wouldn't give credit where credit was due. In the holy name of Jehovah they bowed to a cow then boldly dropped trou.'

---

[1] Exodus 32:22
[2] Genesis 3:12

Section III
Law

"Wherefore then serveth the law? It was added be-
cause of transgressions, till the seed should come to
whom the promise was made" (Galatians 3:19a).

Law: [Greek, nomos] regulation, principle, standard for the
administration of justice.

God's law is not introduced in scripture until you get
to Exodus 20. But you will find a host of sins leading up to
the issuing of the law. Cain missed the mark at the altar
when he presented his measly offering there. God tried to
work with him but he just grew uglier and eventually killed
his brother. Cain paid a hefty price for that sin even though
there were no official laws on the books. God also judged
immorality with a global flood prior to the written law.
Sodom was judged before sodomy was outlawed. God exe-
cuted judgment on a whole host of folks before speaking to
Moses from Mount Sinai. Why? For one simple reason:

man knew better. Man knew the difference between good and evil way before the Ten Commandments were etched in stone. Law didn't create sin; it simply drew attention to it.

While God's laws are helpful in protecting us from one another, they serve a much higher purpose. They measure the distance between man and his Maker. Sin creates distance while law only reads the distance. This is not so God can gauge things, but so we can. Law shows the lawbreaker he is far from where he needs to be. But law cannot correct this distance. It offers only an appraisal. You may want to think of the law as a thermometer. It can show you that you're sick and maybe even the degree of your sickness, but a thermometer cannot make you well. No doctor will tell you, "Take two thermometers and call me in the morning." Once we get our reading from the thermometer, we look to the physician to make us well. This is exactly how the law works. We have a Great Physician who desperately wants to heal us. Not only does He desire to heal us, He longs to befriend us. He has gone through great measures to bring us into fellowship with Himself. Yet sin keeps us poles apart! We wouldn't fully realize this if weren't for the law.

Once Moses came down the mountain, he quickly saw how sickly the nation of Israel was. Furthermore, he realized how far from God it was. The law showed him that. And it pointed him back to the Great Physician.

Chapter 4
Whose Side Are You On?

"And when Moses saw that the people were naked; (for Aaron had made them naked unto their shame among their enemies:) Then Moses stood in the gate of the camp, and said, 'Who is on the LORD's side? let him come unto me.' And all the sons of Levi gathered themselves together unto him" (Exodus 32:25-26)

Once Moses returned to camp and witnessed the shameful behavior of his people firsthand, he pulverized the golden calf. He made the golden flakes into moo-juice powder, dumped it in the river then forced the Israelites to lap it up.[1] (This is the only calf-inated beverage ever mentioned in scripture!) Next Moses called for an allegiance to the Lord. Only one tribe stepped up, the tribe of Levi. The Levites were then given authority to execute judgment on

---

[1] Exodus 32:20

the 11 unrepentant tribes. Three-thousand people fell that day. That's the wages of sin – death! The only way to avoid it is to stand with God. The Levites who valiantly stood with God entered into His blessings and were made priests. The others weren't so fortunate.

Though it was an ill-fated attempt to shrug Moses off, Aaron wasn't kidding when he said the people were set on mischief. This statement represents an undeniable truth concerning all of mankind. The prophet Jeremiah expresses it this way, *"The heart is deceitful above all things, and desperately wicked: who can know it?"* (Jeremiah 17:9) Though laws fail to change the heart, they are effective in controlling behavior. That's because laws demand account-ability. They also assure consequences for the uncoopera-tive! Therefore, laws keep people in check. Without them society loses control, as we see in the case of the lawless children of Israel. I thank God that I live in a country with traffic laws. If it were not for these rules and the enforce-ment thereof, our roads would be an utter mess. Not long ago I visited Kampala, a bustling city in Uganda. Traffic was bumper to bumper. I saw no road signs of any kind. As for me, I would never get behind the wheel of a car in Kampala without fearing for my life. The roads there are complete chaos.

Traffic laws may control chaos but they have little im-pact on the heart. I know this first hand. Though the sign on the interstate may say 70 MPH, in my heart I've got the peddle to the metal. No officer is going to pull me over for what's in my heart. God will, though. He does see the heart. Consider the Pharisees. They were all sticklers for the law. Their outward behavior was well controlled. But our Lord didn't cut them any slack whatsoever. He called them 'hypocrites' and 'white-washed tombs' because their hearts were so corrupt. Jesus also taught:

"Ye have heard that it was said by them of old time, Thou shalt not commit adultery: But I say unto you, That whosoever looketh on a woman to lust after her hath committed adultery with her already in his heart" (Matthew 5:27-28).

The lesson is clear, if it's just some law keeping us from sin, and not our own conscience, we're guilty. Who we are is what we are on the inside, not the outside. The Exodus story affirms this. Why did the Levites receive blessing and the other tribes receive punishment? After all, they were all guilty of the same sin! The reason is this: the Levites had a change of heart while the others did not.

Without exception, God offers an opportunity for a change of heart. He is known to wait a very long time. Once that window of repentance opens, we must choose which side to stand on. All of Israel, save the tribe of Levi, remained where they were. Gulping down the powdered moo-malt wasn't enough to 'shake' them. Moses knew they would eventually have to face the moo-zik. It wasn't the law that worried Moses. He had pulverized that, too! Israel's prophet knew that these were a stiff-necked people with calloused hearts. Though the law might control them, it could never save them. What the law did for Moses was give him an accurate reading of how far Israel was from God. His only recourse was to plead for mercy. So he went back up the mountain, reasoning that it would be easier to change the heart of God than the hearts of his kinsmen.

The day following the crude cow carnival Moses told the unrepentant idolaters, *"Ye have sinned a great sin: and now I will go up unto the LORD; peradventure I shall make an atonement for your sin"* (Exodus 32:30). It was a gracious offer on Moses' part to pay for the sins of Israel. But what possibly could he have given God that would have covered the iniquities of an entire nation? As noble as his intentions were, Moses was too bankrupt to pay for his own sins. The other aspect to this was that Israel was totally un-repentant. Its debt would continue to pile up with countless more sins. There is just no possible way proud man can be reconciled to God so long as he remains in rebellion. To quote the apostle James, *"God resisteth the proud, but giveth grace unto the humble"* (James 4:6).

Thankfully we live in an age where the sin of man is all paid up. The debt was taken care of by the only One qualified to pay it because He is absolutely sinless. Jesus Christ paid the full price of our iniquities with His own precious blood on Calvary. The last words uttered from the cross were, "It is finished." Jesus actually used accounting terminology meaning, "Paid in full." Our Lord left no out-standing balance. He did not say, "Down payment made," or "First installment submitted." He did not leave us with a balance due where we pick up the rest of the tab through works or religion. All our sins were paid in full at the cross. What holds true for Moses holds true for each of us. We are too spiritually bankrupt to pay for our own sins. There is nothing we can do to cover them. So, Jesus paid the price for us. Yet even today God still resists the proud. We either stand on His side or we stand on the side of sin. Choosing sin will keep us separated from God. The law will serve as an ever present reminder that we are far from Him. I won't beat around the bush; unless you have a change of heart your sins will kill you. God, however, stands ready to for-give. Salvation is but a step away. Will you stand on the Lord's side?

Section IV
Separation

"I am cast out of thy sight" (Jonah 2:4).

"But now in Christ Jesus ye who sometimes were far off are made nigh by the blood of Christ" (Ephesians 2:13).

Separation: [Webster's Dictionary] *not connected, being apart*

In the second chapter of his short booklet, Jonah offers a chilling look inside the belly of a fish. He compares his brief stay crammed in this slimy creature as a literal hell. While the imagery is frightful, the most disturbing commentary he gives is, *"I am cast out of thy sight!"* (Jonah 2:4) This was our Lord's greatest agony as He hung from the cross. It wasn't the crown of thorns, his open wounds or even His nail-pierced hands that caused Him to wail from that tree. The greatest torment of Christ is revealed in this one excruciating cry: *"My God, my God, why have you for-*

saken me?"[1] For the first time in eternity, Christ experienced separation from the Father as the sins of the world piled upon Him. What He had dreaded most and what caused Him to sweat crimson bullets in the garden was now being realized in proportions no mortal man can ever fully fathom. In that one haunting moment, God had no choice but to turn away from His Only Begotten because He cannot look upon sin. For Christ, it was more than He could bear even for a split second. And to be separated from God for all eternity is more than any soul can ever bear. Man can endure physical pain. We can overcome mental anguish. But the wailing and gnashing of teeth in Hell is not because of the fiery flames. It is the sheer torment of total separation from God. Imagine no hope and no Light, only the frightful realization of being lost in utter darkness for all eternity. This is what Christ came to save us from!

---

[1] Matthew 27:46 & Psalm 22:1

Chapter 5
Take the Honey and Run

"And the LORD said unto Moses, 'Depart, and go up hence, thou and the people which thou hast brought up out of the land of Egypt, unto the land which I swore unto Abraham, to Isaac, and to Jacob, saying, Unto thy seed will I give it: And I will send an angel before thee; ...Unto a land flowing with milk and honey: for I will not go up in the midst of thee; for thou art a stiffnecked people: lest I consume thee in the way'"
(Exodus 33:1-3).

God's Word would not amount to much if He were wishy-washy with His promises. Even if we don't hold up our end of the deal He must hold up His. King David understood this when he declared, *"Forever, O LORD, thy word is settled in heaven"* (Psalm 118:89). We see this in God's dealings with the Israelites. The Lord vowed to get them to the Promised Land and He will. They don't deserve milk and honey, but they shall have it. In time it will once again slip through their fingers, but that will be their own doing. The same holds true for all of us. God is faithful to pour His blessings, yet we allow them to slip from our grubby little paws. He promises peace, joy, wisdom and rest; all the while we dodge Him like a bullet. I liken God's blessing unto a gushing waterfall. It unloads on some while others only get splashed. There are also those who barely get a trickle; the reason being -- they are just too far away. You see, friend, this heavenly shower falls upon a certain Rock. If you are standing upon the Rock you will enjoy the fullness of God's blessings. If you're standing elsewhere, you'll miss them. But, true to His word, God's blessings are constantly flooding down. We may walk away from them, but they continue to pour regardless. They'll still be there when we return. The more centered we are on the Rock the more blessed we will be.

Make no mistake; there are perks that come with God's presence. Deep down we know this. Should we dare check out on the Lord, the last thing we would ever want to hear Him say would be, "You're on your own now!" This was the case with Israel. God would, however, remain true to His word. He would see to it that the elect get to the Holy Land. But there is a slight change of plans. God's presence would not go with them. He is not one to force His presence on anyone. If we want space, He allows it. He doesn't go anywhere He is not welcome. If His presence is welcome, He must be invited. When it comes to idolaters, it is in their best interest He not join them. God would have no other alternative but to smoke them. The question at this point is -- what exactly does it mean when God withdraws His presence? This needs to be asked in light of the fact that scripture teaches that God is omnipresent, meaning He is everywhere at all times. How does one reconcile God's presence with God's absence? When He resists us it means that we cannot experience intimacy, communion or fellowship with Him. Sin has separated us and removed us from His hedge of protection. If we're bowing before a cow, we won't find God warming up to us. His Spirit departs. We are no longer in a place where He can bless us. The milk and honey may be there but it won't be as sweet. It won't satisfy.

The Lord offered two reasons why He would not join Israel on their trip. Firstly, He told them they were a *stiff-necked people* meaning they were stubborn, proud and uncooperative. They were stuck in their ways. Their hearts were hard and needed to be broken. The other reason God gave for not joining the Israelites was He'd have to consume them if He did. Pulling out was an act of mercy on the Lord's part. He would have to judge these calf-wits if He remained in their company. However, withdrawing from them held the hope of shaking them back to their senses. You see, God would rather restore His people than destroy them.

Consider the parable of the prodigal son.[1] In this story told by Jesus, a young man wants to collect early on his inheritance. He is freely given all that was promised him. The prodigal packs up and quickly leaves his father's presence for a life of debauchery and womanizing. The father does not go with him. Imagine if he did! Dad would have dealt very harshly with this rascal! But that is not what happens. Father allows son to bail with his cut of milk and honey and then waves him off. The foolish lad squanders his bounty on booze and babes, and before long he is mooching for pig-slop. That's when he finally realizes how blessed he was under his father's care. In his case, absence does make the heart grow fonder. He runs home to papa where he is received back with open arms. Jesus obviously told this parable to illustrate our heavenly Father's love for us. Yes, when we are rebellious He lets us go. He does not

---

[1] Luke 15:11-24

go with us. The fellowship is severed. Yet He waits for our return with the hopes we will long for His presence once again. When we do come back, He always welcomes us with open arms. Do you see how merciful God is? Even when He withdraws His presence it is for our own good. His intent is to see us restored. And for man to be restored he must first be broken, so God allows him time in the pig sty.

The lesson of the prodigal agrees with what Paul wrote to the church at Corinth. (See 1 Corinthians 5.) In this uncompromising letter, the apostle addresses some hanky-panky between a young man and his step-mother. Because this fellow was unrepentant Paul charged, *"...deliver such a one unto Satan for the destruction of the flesh, that the spirit may be saved in the day of the Lord Jesus"* (1 Corinthians 5:5). This wayward lamb was to be denied the privilege of Christian fellowship. While some might say excommunication is a rather harsh position, these same bleeding hearts would have only contributed to this man's ultimate destruction. The truth of the matter is, Paul's directive served to shake this immoral brother back to his senses. In his second letter to the Corinthian church Paul writes, *"Sufficient to such a man is this punishment, which was inflicted of many. So that contrariwise ye ought rather to forgive him, and comfort him, lest perhaps such a one should be swallowed up with overmuch sorrow. Wherefore I beseech you that ye would confirm your love toward him"* (2:6-8). In other words, excommunication had produced its desired results. It was now time to receive back this repentant brother and love him like the dickens.

It is a severe matter indeed when God removes His presence. From what I have gleaned from scripture, it is never His first option but always a last resort. While the heart is still soft, it's His kindness that leads one to repentance. When the heart is cold, it's His absence that leads to repentance. This is how God was forced to deal with the stiff-necked cow worshippers in the Exodus account. How did they react when the Lord said, "I'm pulling out?" They mourned as if someone had died! (See Exodus 33:4.) Once you have truly tasted of God's goodness it is not something you ever wish to lose. A nagging emptiness will eventually have you crawling back. When that day finally comes, the Father will be there… with arms wide open.

Chapter 6
Camp Moses

"And Moses took the tabernacle, and pitched it without the camp, afar off from the camp, and called it the Tabernacle of the congregation. And it came to pass, that every one which sought the LORD went out unto the tabernacle of the congregation, which was without the camp" (Exodus 33:7).

It did not set well with Moses that God withdrew his presence from Israel. But rather than stay around and pitch a fit, he left to pitch a tent. "If the Lord isn't where I'm at," he reasoned, "I'll go after Him." Moses offers a wonderful illustration of what it means to seek hard after God. He had two options: remain at camp without God or leave. His only chance of re-connecting with God was the latter. At the beginning of this section we saw *separation* defined as *"not connected, being apart."* When it comes to our relationship with the Lord, separation is obviously a bad thing. As for our relationship with idolaters, it's a good thing. It's important that we know our place, where we fit in. We've got one plug; it can't be plugged into both the world and God simultaneously. We connect to one or the other. This is the idea behind *holiness*. It means to be "set apart" from the world and to be rightly connected with God. This isn't to say we break off all secular ties. Evangelism wouldn't be possible if that were the case. Like Jesus, we are to be known as friends of sinners. But we're not to plug in where they are. The objective is to swing their plugs over. The Bible gives us a code to live by which states:

> *"Be ye not unequally yoked together with unbe-*
> *lievers: for what fellowship hath righteousness*
> *with unrighteousness? and what communion hath*
> *light with darkness?"* (2 Corinthians 6:14)

We are to love unbelievers. We are to befriend them and reach out to them. We are never to judge or hassle them. But we don't align ourselves with their lifestyle. And when it comes to believers who behave like unbelievers, we are to distance ourselves even further.

> *"But now I have written unto you not to keep*
> *company, if any man that is called a brother be a*
> *fornicator, or covetous, or an idolater, or a railer,*
> *or a drunkard, or an extortioner; with such a one*
> *no not to eat"* (1 Corinthians 5:11).

The above passage identifies the sad predicament where Moses had found himself. He was in the company of brothers who had dragged the name of Jehovah into their ugly sin. So Moses distanced himself from the crowd. He took up his tent and pitched it elsewhere… *far from the camp!*

Moses called his tent the "tabernacle of meeting." It was a place far from distraction and far from all the immorality and idolatry going on at Camp Golden Calf. In this humble tent Moses sought hard after God, the very God who had removed His presence from Israel. The Bible surely says that God rewards those who earnestly seek after Him.[1] We will see wonderful evidence of this truth very soon. Before going there, let us not miss out on the important life-lesson before us. If you are serious about pursuing the Lord, you may have to do as Moses did. It may be time to pull up your stakes and pitch your tent elsewhere. Should you find yourself in a camp where God does not dwell, you would do well to leave. Turn from that place and turn to the Lord. The psalmist declares, *"As the hart panteth after the water brooks, so panteth my soul after thee, O God"* (Psalm 41:1). Is that the cry of your heart? Do you have a longing for God? Seek Him! It paid off for Moses; it will pay off for you.

In the Christian experience, it is the presence of God we live for. It's not about signing off on a long list of rules or following traditions or joining some stuffy organization. Christianity is about one thing – relationship. This is what makes the presence of God so foundational. This is why we pursue Him. And let us not forget, while we were yet sinners He came after us! Some may claim they found God, but the truth is He was never lost. It is God who pursues sinners. But as saints, we must pursue God! And He rewards those who do. Just ask Moses. His big payoff is well recorded in the Exodus story: *"And it came to pass, as Moses entered into the tabernacle, the cloudy pillar descended, and stood at the door of the tabernacle, and the LORD talked with Moses"* (33:9). Moses was indeed rewarded handsomely for his diligence. And there is no higher reward than the very presence of God! Life is absolutely meaningless without it.

---

[1] Hebrews 11:6

Moses' next blessing came in the form of a voice. The Exodus account further tells us, *"And the LORD spoke unto Moses face to face, as a man speaketh unto his friend"* (Exodus 33:11). This is no small prize. In my line of work I deal with people who are often frustrated because they never hear from God. But then, they don't take the radical steps Moses did. Should we seek the Lord with like diligence we will most definitely hear from Him. He may not speak with thunder, we may not even hear an audible whisper, but there will be a word from above which penetrates the heart. The question is: are you presently in a place where you can hear His voice? Or is there too much commotion where you've set up camp? Not only did the Lord speak to Moses, He spoke to him personally, as a man speaks to a friend. They didn't dialogue in King James English or in lofty church terms. There was nothing pious about their conversation. It was spontaneous, intimate and real. Moses had something the other Israelites didn't – a relationship with the Lord. God longs for all of us to enjoy this kind of fellowship with Him. Should you detect distance, you may want to consider where you've set up camp.

Section V
Worship

"But the hour cometh, and now is, when the true worshipers shall worship the Father in spirit and in truth: for the Father seeketh such to worship him" (John 4:23).

Worship: [Greek, proskuneo] kiss towards

In our culture we are accustomed to various types of kisses. We may want to keep our distance and blow a kiss. Then there is the friendly peck. This is how I used to kiss my aged grandfather on the cheek. His wrinkly face was smothered with prickly whiskers so the objective was to get in and get out quickly. Then there is the way a man kisses the woman he loves. If he is true, he will kiss no other like this. It is passionate and intimate. It is moist and it lingers. If you were to compare your worship to a kiss, which would it be? Are you one to blow God kisses from a distance? Maybe you prefer a friendly peck -- you like to be quick about it. Or perhaps you are a lingerer; you favor worship that is intimate and passionate. You may be surprised to learn that the word rendered for 'worship' in the New Testament comes from the Greek expression for kissing. Interestingly enough, we do find two types of kisses in the Bible. Paul ends several of his epistles by instructing the brethren to "greet one another with a holy kiss."The word he uses for "holy kiss" is *philema* which refers to a brotherly peck. But this is not how worship is described. This is one of those wet, lingering kisses between two people who are passionate about each other. The New Testament term for worship is *proskuneo* which means "*to kiss towards.*" The *Strong's Greek Dictionary* includes this example: *like a dog licking his master's hand.* This gives us an idea of how intimate the act of worship should be. True worshipers are passionate. They linger in God's presence for as long as possible. For the true worshipper this is the highest form of spiritual intimacy one can experience. It goes way beyond emotionalism and transcends tradition. It's sweet. It's sincere. The Father is looking for such people to worship Him because they are passionate about seeking Him. They are passionate about His presence. And they're not wasting time kissing up to cows.

Chapter 7
Worship From Afar

"And all the people saw the cloudy pillar stand at
the tabernacle door: and all the people rose up
and worshiped, every man in his tent door"
(Exodus 33:10).

Before we venture any further into the subject of worship, let's talk about heaven. People have different ideas about what it will be like. If you are a surfer, you might imagine that you'll catch the ultimate wave up there. Maybe you're a skier and have visions of a never ending slope of pure powder. Or is it golf that you enjoy and you think heaven will offer the seamless playing field of green? Personally, I can't imagine competitive sports in a perfect paradise. As enjoyable as they can be, there is generally a loser when it comes to competition. The idea of "losers" in heaven doesn't register well with me. Truthfully, we just don't know what kind of activities heaven will offer. We do know that it will be better than anything we've ever enjoyed. If it so happens there aren't any surfboards or golf clubs beyond the pearly gates, they won't be missed. Even if there are such things, we'll be tossing them aside to bask in the Lord's presence.

Scripture offers only a few snapshots of heaven. In each instance we see the same activity – worship! The prophet Isaiah was privileged enough to catch a glimpse of heaven and that is what he saw.[1] Likewise, when the Apostle John caught a sneak peek of paradise he saw the same thing.[2] Though we do not know a lot about the hereafter, one thing we do know for certain is the Lord will be seated high upon His throne where He will be worshipped by all who adore Him! As for me, I hope to be numbered among them. Now, maybe that sounds fanatical to some or boring to others. "What about the ski boats and fishing poles?" they protest. I will answer with a statement that may not make me very popular. Yet at the risk of what others may think I'll say it anyway. *If there is something you enjoy more than worship, then you have never fully entered in.* Once true worship happens, there is no place you'd rather be. On the other hand, when worship is reduced to a religious routine, this indicates distance between the worshipper and the One worshipped. This surely seems to be the case with the Israelites of Moses' day.

The Exodus story tells us that anyone who wanted to seek the Lord went to the tent where Moses was. It seems there were very few takers who actually did this. Most were content to pay their respects from afar. Indeed, they were quite blown away by God's presence upon the tabernacle of meeting. Out of reverence many went face down. Sadly, all this was done from a distance. They blew kisses to God from their tent doors at Camp Cow Cow. Moses, on the other hand, lingered in the Lord's presence. Not so with the

---

[1] Isaiah 6:1-3
[2] Revelation 4

rest of his clan. They could only enjoy His presence as spectators. Make no mistake, they were a religious bunch. But religion doesn't get you close to God. Just ask any Pharisee! They worshipped hours on end in the town square but remained far from the Lord. Even when He walked among them, they maintained their distance. Do you know why they didn't recognize Christ? They weren't seeking Him. Seeking God will get you into His presence every time. Religion will not. God desires intimacy.

In the *Book of Revelation* Jesus addresses a body of lukewarm churchgoers at Laodicea. (See Revelation 3:14-22.) These religious hum-drums had no passion for God whatsoever. They were neither hot nor cold, and it was enough to make our Lord want to vomit. It was to these churchy folk Jesus said, *"Behold, I stand at the door, and knock: if any man hear my voice, and open the door, I will come in to him, and will sup with him, and he with me"* (3:20). While this verse is often quoted at evangelical crusades, it was initially directed to Christians... religious, churchy, lukewarm Christians. These dull, deadbeat disciples had lost their zeal for God. If there was any worship going on, which there probably was, Jesus was left completely out of it. Yet He wanted back in. Jesus paints a picture of Himself standing at the door knocking while He waits for a personal invitation to come inside. One thing He will not do is barge His way in. He patiently waits for an open door.

There is a wonderful promise for those who let Jesus in. He promises communion. Jesus said, *"I will come in to him, and will sup with him, and he with me."* Those who lived in New Testament times understood exactly what was meant by this, whereas many today miss the significance altogether. Dining back in Jesus' day was a very intimate experience. There was no personal space. Mealtime was a full contact event. Everyone sat on a common couch where they leaned on each other. There were no individual place settings and hands were favored over utensils. Everyone pulled from a common meat entrée and picked from a shared loaf. There was a lot of double-dipping too. Each dipped their bread into the same bowl. By the way, do you remember Jesus pouring each of the apostles their own goblet of wine at the last supper? It didn't happen. Everyone shared. Dining was a time of communion, people coming together as one. Because the experience was so intimate, people were very selective about whom they ate with. For example, Jews never ate with Gentiles, Samaritans or those dreaded tax collectors. In contrast, we find Jesus extending His invitation to anyone. He doesn't care who you are or where you're from or what you've done. If you open the door, He will commune with you. That's His promise.

Is He knocking on the door of your heart?

Chapter 8
Should I Stay or Should I Go?

"And he [Moses] turned again into the camp"
(Exodus 33:11b).

Moses went the distance to seek the Lord. He did so with diligence and determination. These disciplines are not so uncommon when it comes to carnal pursuits. Most run after sin with great zeal. In my youth I would scale down a steep, rocky hillside to a private little beach in Malibu to join up with some very free-spirited stoners. Malibu was over an hour drive from my house. And if my car wasn't working, I'd hitchhike the full distance! Do you remember the distances you would go? We pursued sin with amazing fervor, didn't we? We didn't fall into temptation... we leaped over hills and dells to it! If we would only seek God with like passion we would have the ultimate worship experience. What lengths are you willing to go to pursue the Lord? What inconveniences are you willing to allow? What sacrifices are you willing to make? We must be prepared to step beyond our own tent doors, beyond our comfort zones and beyond the familiar crowd of "happy campers" if we are truly to be considered seekers of God.

Moses was one who did enjoy the ultimate worship experience. He took radical steps to pursue God. He left his world behind. He went far outside the camp. But… he never stayed away for too long. He had a job to do. That job was back at camp. Moses did not neglect his responsibilities as Israel's leader. He did not remain at the spout where the glory comes out. Oh, how he would have loved to. It could not have been easy for this fellow to leave that place of perpetual blessing. But Moses was a man with a mission. Disobedience to his divine call would have surely altered his communion time for the worse. God's presence is a fearful thing when we resist His will. *"Woe is me,"* said Isaiah when he saw the Lord, *"I am a man of unclean lips."*[1] Isaiah also experienced God's touch in a wonderful way. But he didn't dare linger too long in the presence of Glory. Responding immediately to the Lord's call he cried, *"Send me!"*[2] Isaiah would not milk his private worship time at the expense of others. He sought to strike a balance. Moses also had to juggle his priorities. Time in the tabernacle was not to take away from his time with people. Likewise, time with people was not to take away from his time in the tabernacle. Do you ever feel like that, pulled from two sides? I do. It's a tough balance and we can't afford to compromise on either end. Moses realized he could not effectively minister to others unless he spent time with God. On the other hand, had Moses spent all his time in the tabernacle, he would have compromised his call.

Seeking God's presence must take top priority in our lives. It needs to be our first order of business each day. We should never rush our time with God; it's best to linger. But

---

[1] Isaiah 6:5
[2] Isaiah 6:8

we must be careful not to linger too long. If we are truly listening to His voice we will hear those familiar words, "Whom shall I send?" Hopefully our response will be, "Send me!" Sadly, for some the cost is too high. They don't want to be inconvenienced or disturbed from their TV time. If only they knew the blessings they were missing. It is also possible to go the opposite extreme. We can get so wrapped up in our private worship experience that we no longer have time for anyone else. We become like the guy who spends too long in the Jacuzzi. Had he climbed out sooner he would have felt invigorated. But he'd rather stew in his own stench. Instead of being refreshed he's a smelly, lethargic blob. Worshippers also run the risk of overextending their stay at the Lord's fount. What begins as exaltation can quickly turn to exfoliation. That's when our flaky flesh emerges to the surface. God says, "Come to the fount!' But He also says, "Go! Go, and invite others!" Unless we're willing to go when God tells us, we're simply stewing in our own exfoliation.

It is also true that we can busy ourselves in Christian service so much that our devotion time is greatly compromised. We "go" and never come back to get refreshed. When this happens, we are no longer serving from God's abundance. This inevitably leads to weariness and burn-out. Some may grow increasingly disgruntled as they work so hard and receive such little thanks. Of course, at this stage, it's the pats on the back that keep you going. Once they stop, you stop. The great commission is not to get busy and work hard. We are called to simply pour out what God pours in. Unless we are spending time in God's presence, we are nothing but empty vessels. We have nothing to pour out. As a result, we feel spiritually tapped. When I'm dry in the ministry, it's generally because I'm not allowing God to pour in. I'm running on an empty tank. But when God pours in, I'm on constant overflow without ever feeling drained. This is why I seek the Lord at the beginning of the day. Otherwise I'm running on smelly fumes.

The Lord dealt with the busy church of Ephesus on this issue. (Refer to Revelation 2:1-7.) These saints were workaholics when it came to Christian service. Jesus told them, *"I know your works, your labor..."* He went on to say, *"You have endured... and have not grown weary."* But the Lord wasn't impressed by all their busyness. He was prepared to pull out; He even threatened to do so if things didn't change. Why? As active as these church workers were, they weren't seeking God's presence. God wasn't in anything they were doing in spite of how spiritual things appeared on the surface. Listen to how our Lord rebukes them, *"I have this against you: The love you had at first is gone."* I can't imagine a bigger pill to swallow. That had to have been a hammer for these busy bees. It hammers me every time I read it! It's a constant reminder that we must cultivate a relationship with the Lord each and every day.

Finding that balance between "come" and "go" is something that must be mastered in marriage too. If a husband doesn't spend time with his wife, their relationship will surely suffer. They will lose that sense of intimacy. They will grow distant as friends. On the other hand, if a husband never leaves his wife's side, he will fail as a leader in every other area of his life. At some point he must "go" to work and provide for his family. He must "go" spend time with his children and invest in their lives as well. It would be far too selfish for him to linger in the presence of his wife all day. Each of us must find that balance in our spiritual walks as well. He says to us "come," therefore we seek Him. Then we linger in His presence until He says "go." But we need to be listening in order to hear what He is telling us.

Section VI
Relationship

Relation [*Webster's Dictionary*] *connection*

One can learn a lot from a dictionary. I did. Or maybe a light clicked on that wasn't on before. *Webster's* definition of "separation" is: *not connected.* The definition Webster offers for "relation" is: *connection.* Did a light just click on for you, too? Speaking of light, let's use a bulb to illustrate what all this means. Bulbs don't initially give off light once you pull them out from the box. As long as they remain separate from the power source, there is nothing illuminating about them at all. A relationship is required. A circuit must be formed. Once the bulb gets into the loop, energy flows. This connection causes oneness which is reflected through light. Without this connection, that bulb is nothing more than a fragile, empty shell. What gives it usefulness is the source it is plugged into. I'm sure you're already making the *connection* by now. The light for us doesn't come on until we tap into the true source of Light.

Without Him we remain dull, empty and fragile. However, once we are one with Him, things look a whole lot brighter.

Man enters this world disconnected from God. Adam and Eve were the first to pull the plug when they enjoyed their little fruit snack. Sin has kept us disconnected ever since. The Bible is God's story of how He has attempted to reconnect with mankind and how we have continually resisted Him. We have seen some religious efforts and even acts of reverence from Camp Cow Cow in the Exodus story. But the Israelites still remain disconnected from God up to this point. However, we do see at least one person connecting: Moses! We will now see how this connection ignites into a brilliant relationship.

Chapter 9
Friend of God

*"And the LORD spoke unto Moses face to face, as
a man speaketh unto his friend"* (Exodus 33:11a).

Jesus seemed to use the term "friend" quite freely. When it was reported that Lazarus was in grave condition Jesus informed His disciples, *"Our friend Lazarus sleepeth."*[1] When Judas showed up to betray Jesus He asked, *"Friend, why are you here?"*[2] Jesus called his apostles friends and He was called "friend of sinners," Though Jesus used the term "friend" quite freely, it was never meant to be taken lightly. Friendship as defined in scripture transcends way beyond the casual. It seems that in Bible times the water of friendship was thicker than the blood of siblings. Solomon stated, *"A friend loveth at all times, and a brother is born for adversity"* (Proverbs 17:17). He went on to say, *"There is a friend that sticketh closer than a*

---

[1] John 11:11
[2] Matthew 26:50

brother" (Proverbs 18:24). Lest you think the dear king was a jewel shy of a crown, remember it was Jesus who said, *"Greater love hath no man than this, that a man lay down his life for his friends"* (John 15:13).

There are only two Old Testament figures referred to in scripture as friends of God. One is Moses, the other is Abraham. When Jesus was called "friend of sinners," the idea was that He had befriended some very messy people. No doubt He had! To be known as a "friend of God" suggests something different. With respect to Abraham and Moses, these two sinners had befriended the Lord! James explains in his epistle, *"Abraham believed God, and it was imputed unto him for righteousness: and he was called the Friend of God"* (2:23). I find this absolutely refreshing. All it took for Father Abe to be a friend of God was belief. It wasn't religious works or living a perfect life. Friendship with God was achieved through pure and simple faith. Abraham believed God's promises and instantly became His bosom-buddy. One thing about faith, it can't sit still. It's as though faith has legs. If we truly trust God, faith will carry us closer to Him. We clearly see this with Abraham. His was a pilgrimage marked by a trail of altars. Then there is Moses. While the rest of the Israelites were steered to a hand-carved calf, faith moved Moses into the presence of God. This took their relationship to a very deep and personal level. God and Moses connected and became close pals.

The Lord has no problems whatsoever with befriending sinners. He'll hang out with just about anybody. There isn't some high standard we have to meet. There aren't any hoops to jump through. A checkered past won't disqualify anyone. The only criterion is faith. You must trust Him, that's all. Believe in the Lord. Believe in His promises. Believe He rewards those who diligently seek after Him. And you too will be a friend of God.

Chapter 10
Known By Name

"Yet thou hast said, I know thee by name" (Exodus 33:12).

It was a time when God and His people were no longer on speaking terms. The Israelites weren't speaking to the Lord; He wasn't speaking to them. God checked out of the camp while the cow crusaders stalled behind. Deity and humanity remained worlds apart. Though God was far from His people, He wasn't far from sight. Occasionally some would capture a peek of Glory from their tent doors, but they maintained their distance. Few pursued the Lord. Those who did rode on the coattails and passion of Moses. Moses led the way. Moses erected the tent. Moses alone cried out to God. And God spoke to Moses. As far as the record shows, God spoke only to Moses. And somewhere in that divine discourse the Lord told him, "I know you by name." Does this sound like a peculiar thing for the "All-knowing" to say? As if there are some names the omniscient One isn't yet familiar with? Or does He forget? After all, He is pretty old. It has to be asked, does He know your name? Does He know mine? What does it mean when God says, "I know you by name?"

I grew up in a neighborhood full of kids. This was back in the day when *X-Box* and *Play Station* were unheard of even by the Jetsons. Back then, people actually knew their neighbors and kids played outdoors! The boys I hung out with were interested in only two things: pretty girls and fast cars. Most of us were too young to date or drive, but we admired the older kids who could. I'll never forget cool Larry. He wore the cool Elvis shades and had a cool Elvis hairdo. And Larry had the slickest ride ever. It was a bright yellow, cherried out '56 Chevy wagon with sparkling chrome trim and shiny Mag rims. None of us really knew Larry personally, we just knew of him because he would drive down our street quite often. When he did, our envious eyes followed as if Larry were some kind of superhero. My brother, Rick, would always wave to our hero when he passed by. "That's Larry," he'd tell us, "He's a friend of mine." Knowing someone so cool made my brother worthy of admiration as well. I still remember the day Larry stopped to speak to Rick. Rick had waved to him as he always had. "Hi Larry!" he called out. Larry signaled for him to approach the car window. The rest of us followed close behind. We just had to hear what our hero might say to my big brother. With everyone well within earshot Larry said, "Hey, kid, what's your name?" We all laughed hysterically when it was finally discovered that Rick and Larry weren't really friends at all. They had never even met! Many of us relate to the Lord just like my brother related to Larry. They may know His name or look up to Him as if He were a superhero. They may even wave to Him from the curbside like Rick did, or from the tent door like the Israelites. But God is asking the same question as cool Larry, "Hey, kid, what's your name?"

To know someone by name speaks of a close relationship. I know quite a few people, but I'm not on a first name basis with all of them. Some I know as Mister or Miss. Others I might refer to as Doctor or Professor. I may address a gentleman as Sir or a lady as Ma'am if we are not well acquainted. But I would never refer to my wife as such. I know her by name. To call her ma'am or miss would only create distance in our relationship. When I was in my twenties and thirties I served as a youth pastor. The teenagers in my church all knew me as Terry. One evening after youth group, one of the gals informed me that she had to start calling me Mr. Michaels. In spite of my objections, her parents insisted upon it. I was extremely uncomfortable with this formality for a couple of reasons. For one, I had never been addressed this way before. And, honestly, I wasn't ready for unnecessary titles that would only serve to remind me I was nearing middle age. Admittedly, there may have been some vanity on my part. But the bigger issue was -- I had been on a first name basis with this gal and her family for several years. The idea of her suddenly calling me Mr. Michaels was quite awkward. I felt this requirement would only create distance. I was relieved when her folks finally reconsidered their position. I don't mean to discourage proper decorum. It is important that young people address elders appropriately. But if the elder prefers to be called by name, that also should be honored.

Just as I know my children by name, our Heavenly Father knows His children by name. If you are a child of God, He knows you by name. And that name is recorded in the Book of Life forever! If your name does not appear in the Book of Life, it is because God does not know you. Certainly He knows of you and everything about you. He knows every hair on your head! But He does not know you intimately on a personal level. Nor do you know Him, should this be the case. We are either separated from God or connected to Him, strangers or friends. The only way we can truly connect with the Father is through His Son. We must call upon the name above all names, Jesus Christ. The instant we do a relationship is formed. No longer are we estranged from God; we are embraced as children and He calls us by name.

There are wonderful privileges associated with being a child of God. The Book of Romans tells us, *"Ye have received the Spirit of adoption, whereby we cry, Abba, Father"* (8:15). God is not just a father to us He is *Abba, Father*, or as we would say today in our culture, "Daddy, Father." The title "Father" reminds us of who God is with regard to position. He is an authority figure. "Daddy" is altogether different. This is a term of endearment which speaks of relationship. There are many fathers in the world, but not all are daddies. Not all fathers enjoy a close relationship with their children. I am reminded of the Disney classic *Mary Poppins*. Those poor children, who Ms. Poppins became nanny to, were very distant from their father. They did not know him as Daddy. Whenever he entered the house the kids stood at attention in their proper little outfits while their father read them the riot act. You never saw these little rascals climb onto Daddy's lap or wrap their arms around his neck. They did not know him in an intimate way. Our Heavenly Father longs for us to know Him intimately. He's not just the big man with a gavel in one hand and a rule book in the other. He is the Daddy with arms wide open ready to receive us into His wonderful presence. And He calls us by name.

Chapter 11
Finding Grace

"Yet thou hast said, I know thee by name, and thou hast
also found grace in my sight"
(Exodus 33:12).

The Lord addresses separation through the administration of the law. He deals with relationship through the dispensation of grace. In this way, He is a great role model for anyone who has kids. There is the Father side of God who implements guidelines, accountability and correction. There is also the daddy side of God who lavishes us with grace upon grace. In short, there is law for those who are far and favor for those who are near. In the Exodus story, the Israelites stray far from God, but the long arm of the law quickly catches up with them. They are held accountable for their actions and are corrected in the measure to which they deserve. Moses, on the other hand, finds grace, which is more than he deserves. It is not a difficult thing to find grace. Wherever God is, there it shall be. All one need do is seek Him. That's all Moses did. And God rewarded him handsomely for it. He rewarded him with grace upon grace.

The difference between the Old Testament and the New can be expressed in one word – grace! The Old Testament was God showing man that His favor is impossible to earn through human effort. The New Testament offers God's favor through simple faith. Jeremiah spoke of a day when the Old Covenant would be replaced by the New and religion would be kicked to the curb by relationship.[1] This relationship would not be founded upon law but upon love, and religious works would be overshadowed by the pure wonder of God.

> *"For they shall all know Me from the least of them to the greatest of them, says Jehovah. For I will forgive their iniquity, and I will remember their sins no more"* (Jeremiah 31:34).

Moses was permitted to experience such wonder in a time of utter darkness. This glorious foretaste of God's coming promise left Him begging for more, as we shall see more clearly in upcoming chapters. Moses seems to have caught on to the fact that the new covenant would one day be fulfilled through the very people who bowed before the golden calf. Why did God choose them? Grace!

Grace is God giving us what we are unworthy of. It secures our place in eternity. It is the condition of God's promises and the catalyst for His presence. Grace saves us from judgment, death and hell. Grace saves, not faith, as some might suppose. If it were faith that saved, then we would deserve some credit. But we are not worthy of such praise. God gets all the credit. *"For by grace are ye saved* **through faith***; and that not of yourselves: it is the gift of*

---

[1] Jeremiah 31:31-33

God" (Ephesians 2:8). (Bold print mine.) No doubt, faith is foundational in our experience with God. Faith does not move mountains, though. God does. In faith we trust Him to accomplish the impossible. Faith is the key to knowing God and pleasing Him. It's impossible to please Him any other way.[1] As significant and marvelous as faith is, it cannot save anybody. Only by the grace of God can one be saved. This grace, however, can only be appropriated through faith. It only takes a smidgen. The size of a mustard seed will do. Yes, faith that small will buy you loads of grace. It will free you from the law. It will usher you into God's presence. Without any hoops to jump through, eternity will land right on your lap! There is grace upon grace at our immediate disposal. Dig in. You've been given a shovel called faith.

While the rest of the Israelites were still trying to digest the powdery cow shake and put back the pieces of the law, Moses stepped out in faith. He sought after a God, who seemed to be out of sight and out of touch. Yet Moses was convinced that would all change through faith. The author of Hebrews tells us that faith believes two things: (1) God is and (2) God rewards those who diligently seek after Him (11:6). Following these two principles, Moses landed upon something the other Israelites didn't – amazing grace! Moses found undeserved favor in the sight of God! You will discover it, too. Simply step out in faith. Seek the Lord diligently and discover grace upon grace upon grace.

---

[1] Hebrews 11:6

Section VII
Prayer

"And all things, whatsoever ye shall ask in prayer, believing, ye shall receive" (Matthew 21:22).

Prayer [Author's definition] conversation with God

Though our approaches may vary, there is little debate as to what prayer is. It is the means by which we communicate with our heavenly Father. The question for most is not "What is prayer?" but "How shall I pray?" Even the apostles needed some guidance in this area. Thank goodness, they looked to Jesus for answers.[1] Jesus began His workshop by telling the disciples how not to pray. He told them not to follow the example of the Pharisees who took their loud, lofty prayers wherever they could find an audience. Then there were the pagans who were big on repetitious prayers. Jesus steered the apostles away from this approach

---

[1] Matthew 6:5-15

as well. The Pharisees and the pagans did have one thing in common. In each case their prayers were highly impersonal. Neither group directed their prayers upward. The Pharisees prayed to be idolized while pagans idolized carved images through prayer. Neither can be considered conversation. Idols don't speak, nor do Pharisees listen. I fear this may be true of countless Christians. Many don't allow God to speak, nor are they listening when they pray. A popular prayer in some groups is "my will be done." Though these may not be their exact words, their demands make it clear that this is what they are after. Others favor ancient formula prayers where they recite some canned gibberish over and over again. Both create distance. It is a distance that can only grieve the heart of God. To some extent I understand how He must feel, because I also have children. If my kids only came to me when they wanted something, I'd feel used and unappreciated. Then again, if they recited words not their own over and over again, and that's all I ever heard from them, I would feel unloved. God longs for fellowship. He wants a relationship that is intimate, personal and meaningful. Prayer is not the means by which we gain favor from above. That is why pagans pray, to win some silly god's approval. Faith has already gained us our Lord's approval. Faith has brought us into a right relationship with Him. Now that we're friends we can talk.

Chapter 12
Thy Will Be Done

"Now therefore, I pray thee ... show me now thy way"
(Exodus 33:13).

At this stage in Moses' ministry, I think I know what I would have been praying. My prayer would have gone something like this, "Lord, we tried it Your way and nothing is going well. It's time we start doing things my way!" But that isn't how Moses rolls. He didn't pursue God just so he could demand what he wanted. "Show me now ***Thy*** way," he pleaded. This is consistent with how Jesus taught His disciples to pray. You remember those infamous four words don't you? *Thy will be done!* One cannot truly be seeking God if he is only concerned about getting his own way. Sadly, some camps think this is the priority of prayer. *"Lord, bless me... heal me... grant me... do this... do that... gimme, gimme, gimme!"* Oh, and I almost forgot, *"in Jesus name!"* They cry out as if it were the same as saying *"abracadabra."* Few dare to pray the prayer of

Moses. Seldom do we find like passion for the will of God. Our heavenly Father is often treated like some kind of cosmic errand boy who is expected to jump at our every beck and call. We give him our shopping list, wish list and our "to do" list, then we send Him off without ever taking time to know Him. The "blab it and grab it" crowd is especially guilty of this. They see God as a rich sugar daddy. Their faith is in a blank check, one they fill and forge in the precious name of Jesus.

I've tried imagining my 15-year-old daughter approaching me in this manner. "Father, I claim your car keys in the name of your only son. Release them now unto my hand. I rebuke any spirit that might thwart me from possessing that which I hath declared as mine. Amen and Halleluiah!" This sense of entitlement really cheapens the idea of grace when you think about it. You see, I really do want to give my daughter the car keys at some point in time. But should I comply with her demands, she'll credit her boldness and not my kindness. Furthermore, I would question whether she is ready for the responsibility of driving should she show such blatant disregard for authority. And though she may have all the faith in the world, I'm unmoved by it. I won't surrender the keys until she demonstrates more maturity and humility. My answer will be, "When you're 16, after you've grown up a little, come back then and ask. And lose the proud attitude next time."

Who is little man that we would bark orders at the Lord? Is that how a friend of God behaves? Try even talking to a waitress that way and see how far you get. On second thought, don't. It's not only unfriendly, it's disrespectful. I find that I get much better service when I ask for things politely rather than boss people around. The thing we want to keep in mind when it comes to our God is – He's not our servant! He is our Lord and Master! It seems we should be asking Him, "What would you have me do?" as opposed to telling Him what we think He should do.

When you get right down to it, that's what Moses was declaring when he prayed, "Show me now Thy way." He was submitting himself to the will of the Father, whatever that might be.

I am in no way suggesting that our Father does not like to do nice things for His children. He does. I've walked with Him long enough to know that He is a blessing God. He heals, He gives gifts and He gets things done for people. No argument there. It's the idea of God being treated like a rich sugar daddy that I hope to correct. I also hope some will reconsider how they approach the Lord. Jesus taught us to ask, seek and knock. He didn't say, "bark, bang and bust the door down.": I would challenge anybody to examine each four of the gospels and find one single, solitary instance where someone got their way by barking orders at Jesus. All those who received healings assumed the posture of beggars, every one of them without exception. Here's just one example:

> *"And there came a leper to him, **beseeching** him, and kneeling down to him, and saying unto him, **If thou wilt**, thou canst make me clean"* (Mark 1:40). (Bold print mine.)

This is what we see every time. Whenever we find someone receiving a healing in the gospels the text always says they *beseeched* or *begged* or *pleaded*. They did not bark, shout or demand their way. When these beggars approached Jesus they did so in humility, realizing they were not worthy of what they asked. It wasn't a "name it and claim it" approach. They humbly appealed to our Lord's compassion, grace and kindness. Even Jairus the synagogue ruler assumed the posture of a beggar when he fell before Jesus on behalf of his dying daughter.[1] Then there was the

---

[1] Mark 5:22-23

centurion who was quite accustomed to barking out orders. But he dared not treat Jesus in such a manner. *"I am not worthy that thou shouldest come under my roof,"* the commander told our Lord, *"For I am a man under authority, having soldiers under me: and I say to this man, Go, and he goeth; and to another, Come, and he cometh; and to my servant, Do this, and he doeth it"* (Matthew 8:8-9). Some today would challenge this kind of approach. They would consider it a wimpy demonstration of faith. But listen to Jesus' response to this beggar, *"Verily I say unto you, I have not found so great faith, no, not in Israel"* (Matthew 8:10).

Moses was also a man of great authority. He ranked at the top as Israel's prophet, priest and king. Yet he knew his place before the Lord. In the presence of Greatness, Moses humbled himself. He was stripped of all pride, greed and selfishness. "Your way, Lord," he cried. "What is it? Show me. Show me now!" Is that the cry of your heart? Which do you seek, God's *presents* or God's *presence*? If it is God's presence you are after, seek to know His way. Nothing pleases Him more. And the Lord will be more than glad to show you His way. Once you make this discovery, you'll be more blessed than you ever imagined. These blessings never would have been realized had things gone your way.

> *"But seek ye first the kingdom of God, and his righteousness; and all these things shall be added unto you"* (Matthew 6:33).

Chapter 13
That I May Know You

"Show me now thy way, that I may know thee..."
(Exodus 33:13).

Imagine two friends: one always gets his way while the other continually gives in. Much is known about the one who constantly gets his way. You will know his interests and desires. You will learn what drives, pleases and annoys him. You will discover how he thinks and what makes him tick. You will understand exactly what kind of a man he is, whether wise or a fool. His very soul is exposed for all to see. Little is known about his quiet companion. He remains a complete mystery. The only thing that can be said of him is that he is a total pushover. But one can never really know a fellow like this. Some enjoy the company of pushovers; there is much to gain from them. They become a means to an end. Many treat God the same way. They are not interested in a relationship. They'd rather God just put up and shut up. They prefer distance. To them, God is a complete mystery. He's the polite cloud that patiently waits behind the golden calf. They don't want Him in the way, yet they like Him on call.

The plea of Moses was, *"Show me now thy way."* The purpose of his plea is summed up in these five words: *"that I may know thee."* I wonder how many of us share this longing when we seek God through prayer. Does it ever come down to just that – to know Him? And think about this, who in the entire camp of Israel knew God more intimately than Moses? Were there others who had spent 40 days on a mountaintop with the Lord? Had anyone else heard His voice beckoning from a burning bush? Was there even one other who spoke to God face to face? If anyone knew the Lord, it was our man, Moses! In light of their already close friendship, we must conclude that Moses' real request was to know God more. This one quest seems to sum up the Christian experience altogether. This is why we seek Him, sing of Him, pray to Him and spend time in His Word – to know Him more! Lose this passion and all you have left is a hum-drum, dull religion. You can lump it in with all the others.

Islam teaches that Allah is unknowable. In the Hindu religion there are thousands of gods, yet not one of them is knowable; one simply tries to appease them. This is the chief difference between religion and relationship. Religion asks, "What must I do?" Relationship cries out, "I must know you!" The Christian faith is starkly unique in that we can actually know our God. It is more than just a belief system. It is a journey, an adventure, a divine romance that man begins by befriending the Lord. Each day thereafter becomes yet another opportunity to pursue deeper intimacy with Him.

The fire of any love relationship lies in this never-ending quest – to know the other more. Husbands and wives are well aware of this fact. Once that passion fizzles, the honeymoon is over, the rut has begun. It matters not how many decades a man has been wed to his bride; his marriage is headed for dullsville once he declares, "I know all that I need to know about my wife. I'm done." The journey must continue until one or the other is buried six feet under. Man and wife must incessantly make new discoveries about each other. After 28 years of marriage, I know my wife better than anyone else. I know what pleases her and what irritates her, what makes her laugh and what will make her cry. But I do not know her completely. Nor does she know me completely. Not too long ago, she discovered that I do not care for enchiladas baked in red sauce. After preparing them for me for almost three decades, I finally fessed up to my little secret. I suppose she learned two things about me that day: I don't like tangy foods disguised as Mexican cuisine and, secondly, I can be very long suffering if I really put my mind to it. No one can ever accuse me of not giving those tart little devils a fair chance, that's for sure.

There is much to know about our God. Is eternity even enough time to scratch the surface? As the Lord declared through his prophet Isaiah, *"For as the heavens are higher than the earth, so are my ways higher than your ways, and my thoughts than your thoughts"* (Isaiah 55:9). Paul shared the passion of Moses when he prayed that he might know God. (See Philippians 3:10.) And the apostle prayed for you, dear saint:

"That ye may know what is the hope of his calling, and what the riches of the glory of his inheritance in the saints, And what is the exceeding greatness of his power to us-ward who believe" (Ephesians 1:18, 19).

"And to know the love of Christ, which passeth knowledge, that ye might be filled with all the fullness of God" (Ephesians 3:19).

What new discoveries have you made about the Lord recently? Maybe it was something simple, like, He doesn't really care for prayer beads. He just happens to be patient with those who latch onto them. Or maybe you discovered for the first time (after reading the above passage) that God has an inheritance. An inheritance is a treasure of great worth that an heir looks forward to one day receiving. In this particular case, the heir is God and the treasure is you! Did you know this? If this so happens to be a new revelation, you haven't even scratched the surface. There are so, so many wonderful mysteries we can know about God. Continue your journey by praying the prayer of Moses, "That I may know you." Make this your prayer each day. Set down your wish list and to-do list for awhile and make this your one pure and holy passion – *to know Him more*. Your walk will take an exciting turn. You'll never be the same. You will experience God in a fresh new way. You will know His way. Not only that, you'll love it!

Chapter 14
In His Presence

"My presence shall go with thee" (Exodus 33:14).

It is at the Tabernacle of Meeting where Moses fully realizes the power of intercessory prayer. In that one humble tent, one humble man with one humble prayer turns despair into triumph for an entire nation. Oh, what prayer can do, even a simple utterance lifted by a solitary voice. Previously, we saw how sin had separated Israel from her God. We also saw how God sent His people off to the land of milk and honey without Him. *"For I will not go up in the midst of thee,"* He declared, *"for thou art a stiffnecked people."* We then saw how the Israelites reacted to this bad news; they grieved as if a part of them had died. And now, because one man was courageous enough to rattle the gates of heaven, there is a change of plans. With a simple yet selfless prayer, Moses appeals to the soft side of the Father as he pleads, *"consider that this nation is thy people."* In response, the Lord assures Moses, "I'm going to join you

on that little trip after all!" Perhaps this story sounds re-
markably familiar to your own. Indeed it is the story of
every Christian. We, too, were once separated from God.
Then One like Moses interceded on our behalf.[1] And to a
kingdom of faithful believers our God declares, *"My presence shall go with thee."*

I have heard it asked more than a few times, 'Why
pray when the Lord already knows what we are going to
ask?' Some would answer, "Prayer has a way of getting our
will in sync with His." No doubt, prayer offers this benefit
for those who earnestly seek to know the heart of God. And
though prayer has a subtle way of making us more heavenly minded, I would also submit that it holds an even
higher purpose. Prayer offers us an encounter with His glorious presence that can't be experienced anywhere else, at
least this side of paradise.

Whether it be verbal or silent, "That I may know you"
should be the yearning which lies at the heart of every
prayer uttered. Prayer is the lifeline that keeps us connected
with God's presence. It is the safeguard against separation
from His presence. Those who value the Lord's company
make prayer a top priority. Show me a man who spends
quality time on his knees and I will show you a dear friend
of God. Show me a prayerless Christian and I'll show you
someone who is far from Him. I will also show you someone who struggles with lust, greed and pride. Simply put,
without prayer we haven't got a prayer. Why? We desperately need God's presence in our lives each day! Without it,
the world sucks the life right out of us. We have only one
source for refreshment – the presence of God. Prayer is
what gets us there.

Where did you go today, my friend, and did the Lord
go with thee? Was it a place where the Lord could not go
with thee? And would you have gone there at all had you

---

[1] Deuteronomy 18:15

prayed? God does not join us everywhere we may venture. Yes, He remains in us. He remains in the heart of every believer. But He is not a tag-along. You will find God's presence only when He leads, but He will not follow once we jump in front. He did not join the Israelites around the golden calf. Likewise, there are places we can wander that would sever our fellowship with God. He will not join the married man while he flirts with the secretary. He will not belly up to the bar with the drunken priest. He will not be found at the casino cheering for the missionary. Oh, yes, He is there in Spirit. But there is no fellowship, only distance. How is this fellowship restored? Prayer! Earnest prayer that would haply welcome back the presence of God! Perhaps the following verse will speak to those who might feel distant at this time:

> *"Repent ye therefore, and be converted, that your sins may be blotted out, when the times of refreshing shall come from the presence of the Lord"* (Acts 3:19).

There are those who feel they are in good company because they avoid places of questionable repute. You will not find them in the bars, casinos or theatres. They have found a comfortable spot at the local church. Somehow all the religious rigmarole has them convinced they have God chained by the ankles, and that He's not going anywhere. These religious church-folk are under the false impression that the Lord Almighty resides in a structure. There He waits each week for pious saints to pay Him a visit or two. "At least stop by for the holidays," He is thought to have said. Before we place our trust in the four walls of a sanctuary, let us remind ourselves that God is not happy with every church. You will not find Him in every building that has a steeple or a cross or a dove. He won't be found chillin' behind every stained glass window or tapping His toe to every praise band. Again I am reminded of the Church of Ephesus which Jesus addresses in the second chapter of Revelation. This was a house full of busy bees but it was all superficial churchianity. Jesus warned them that if they didn't get back to the basics of love, He was pulling out. Even in the healthiest of churches not every congregant is experiencing intimacy with the Father. While some may be basking in His presence, others may be as far from Him as the east is from the west. While they may be worlds apart, God is only a prayer away.

Perhaps you find yourself asking "How does one climb out of a religious rut and reclaim lost intimacy?" I know no other way to rekindle these divine affections than to seek His presence. And I know no other way to seek His presence more effectively than prayer. Perhaps you find that your prayer time has grown dull and lifeless. May I be so bold as to ask, what was the purpose of your said prayer time? Did prayer become just another request line, much like the one used to contact the local radio station? Was God like that late night deejay on the other end of the phone line, a likable character you've never really gotten to know? Unless there is that yearning for God's presence, prayer holds little pleasure. We must find that romantic creature within, that adventurous spirit who sees the devotional life as a means of achieving deeper intimacy God. This is when we really start to see things happen. We begin to see the Lord move in marvelous ways. We begin to see where the milk and honey is really at. And best of all we hear the voice of a Friend say, *"My presence shall go with thee."*

Section VIII
Peace

*"Peace I leave with you, my peace I give unto
you: not as the world giveth, give I unto you. Let
not your heart be troubled, neither let it be afraid"*
(John 14:27).

Peace: [Greek, eirene] prosperity, rest, set at one again

We've all looked for it one time or another but peace
could not be found in the world. Maybe you thought a little
extra cash would give you some peace. Perhaps it was the
fancier house, the bigger toys, the better job or the move to
the country. Sure, there was that initial perception of peace,
but how long did it last? How long did it take before you
were in search of something else to bring tranquility to your
life? No, we do not find one ounce of true peace in the
things of this world. The world is where we find frustration,
worry, anxiety, insecurity and instability. I was a happier
camper when I drove old jalopies. I never worried about

them getting scratched or dinged. I lost that peace when I finally upgraded to newer vehicles. The last time I bought a new car right off the lot, somebody put a long scratch on the door with their key. The peace I had invested so much money in lasted less than a week. The world tells us that if we can improve conditions on the outside, we'll be content on the inside. What the world won't tell you is that the contentment it offers is very short lived. It won't be long before you're back with an empty shopping basket begging for your next fix.

"Let not your heart be troubled," says our Lord. He gives peace not as the world gives. The world gives a false sense of peace then quickly takes it back. The peace that God gives is lasting. You may walk away from it but He will never, ever take it back. This peace comes from His presence. When we have the presence of God, all is well on the inside regardless of outside conditions. According to the Strong's Concordance, the New Testament definition for peace is "set at one again." One can never experience true peace so long as he is separated from God. He must be set at one again! The bumper sticker reads true that says, "No God, no peace. Know God, know peace." Peace will never be found in a place, a possession or a paycheck. Lasting peace is only found in one Person, Jesus Christ.

> *"For he is our peace, who hath made both one, and hath broken down the middle wall of partition between us"* (Ephesians 2:14).

Chapter 15
Rest Is the Best

"...and I will give thee rest" (Exodus 33:1).

Why seek the presence of God? For one, you won't find rest anywhere else. When Jesus promised rest for the weary, the condition was, "Come to me."[1] Those who accept find His yoke to be easy and His burden light. What about you? Would you describe your burden as light? Probably not! Let's face it, life is no cake walk. The yoke we've inherited is a grunt and our burdens weigh like an anvil on the back of a small rodent. "It's my cross to bear," one might reason. We feel pushed, pulled and pressured on every side. Even our hearts get crushed. We experience worry, doubt, insecurity, anxiety, panic, fear, pain, guilt, shame, helplessness and hopelessness, headaches and heartbreaks. Need I go on? On top of all this we sweat, toil and labor. Is not the cry of our souls for rest? Couldn't we

---

[1] Matthew 11:28

all use a break? Does the idea of relief appeal to you, my tired friend?

Imagine for a moment how Moses must have felt as the top dog of Israel. He was called to lead between two and three million nags through a barren wilderness. Nothing ever made these grumps happy. Their freedom didn't. Their food didn't. Their Father didn't. These bellyachers were constantly on edge. They spent the bulk of their days whining, complaining and criticizing. This ungrateful bunch couldn't be satisfied for a New York minute. They were stiff-necked, stubborn, uncooperative, non-submissive and disobedient. Moses would have had an easier time leading two million arthritic mules through the Sahara! Do you think, just maybe, that Moses grew weary at times? No doubt he felt an enormous weight of responsibility. And with each passing day his heart must have grown heavier for the people. Assuredly, the proposition of rest was well received by Israel's leader. I imagine it appeals to you as well. And let's be honest, neither you nor I have to put up with a fraction of what Moses had to deal with!

Rest is synonymous with peace. It was the late John Lennon who coined the catchphrase "Give peace a chance." Of course, this began as the anti-war anthem back when we still had troops in Vietnam. Uncle Sam finally did give peace a chance by pulling out of this controversial conflict. But did this decision translate to "inner peace" for anyone? Though I may have sighed with relief when they ended the draft, this was not the beginning of a tranquil existence for yours truly. The sad reality is that we can have utter turmoil on the inside no matter how peaceful things are on the outside. The opposite is also true. We can experience total inner peace even when all hell is breaking loose.

When God promised Moses rest, He wasn't promising a change of outward circumstances. There were no promises to rid his life of all conflict. Nor did the Lord promise to lighten Moses' responsibilities as Israel's leader. On the contrary, the wilderness experience was far from over. Moses' job description would remain the same and he would continue to be surrounded by a melancholy multitude of moaners until the day he died. So what exactly did God promise this poor soul? The Lord offered Moses inner peace! In other words, whatever Moses walked through, no matter how confusing, complicated or chaotic, he would experience rest in God's presence. The same is true for each of us. In a restless world we can rest in Him. This is also what David discovered when he penned:

> *"The LORD is my shepherd; I shall not want. He maketh me to lie down in green pastures: he leadeth me beside the still waters. He restoreth my soul: he leadeth me in the paths of righteousness for his name's sake. Yea, though I walk through the valley of the shadow of death, I will fear no evil: for thou art with me; thy rod and thy staff they comfort me. Thou preparest a table before me in the presence of mine enemies: thou anointest my head with oil; my cup runneth over. Surely goodness and mercy shall follow me all the days of my life: and I will dwell in the house of the LORD forever"* (Psalm 23).

Moses seems to have understood what the Psalmist came to realize. In response to God's promise he replied, *"If thy presence go not with me, carry us not up hence"* (Exodus 33:15). Essentially what Moses said was, "I'd rather be in a desolate desert with You than in a land flowing with milk and honey without You." Do you feel the same way? Would you still pursue the Lord if it meant forfeiting all your milk and honey? Could you rest in material luxury knowing God is not there beside you? I know I couldn't. This is by no means an attempt to make myself sound more spiritual than I actually am. I'm merely saying that the only place I've found true rest is in the presence of God.

The fact that there are as many miserable rich people as there are happy poor people is evidence enough that there is no connection whatsoever between one's peace and one's prosperity. However, should you forsake His presence for the sake of material prosperity, you will lose His peace. This was something Moses wasn't willing to gamble with. Above all else, he desperately longed for God's presence. If that meant dwelling in the desert in utter poverty, he was okay with that. Nothing else mattered but nearness to God. Once a person comes to that place – he can rest!

Section IX
Consecration & Sanctification

"For Moses had said, Consecrate yourselves to-day to the LORD, even every man upon his son, and upon his brother; that he may bestow upon you a blessing this day" (Exodus 32:29).

"And the very God of peace sanctify you wholly; and I pray God your whole spirit and soul and body be preserved blameless unto the coming of our Lord Jesus Christ" (1 Thessalonians 5:23).

Consecration: [Hebrew, mala-yawd] hand-fill. [Riverside Webster's II Dictionary] to dedicate to a specific goal.

Consecration is not the same as sanctification. The two are oftentimes confused because of the close relationship they share. Consecration is a means to an end, the goal being sanctification. Sanctification is an act of God, whereas consecration is something man puts his own mind to. I realize we are using lofty terms here and I don't care for churchy lingo anymore than the next person. Perhaps we can simplify these drab expressions and use everyday language we're all familiar with. We'll start with sanctification. It's just a big, fancy word for "cleanse." I realize we don't often use it in that context much. When I head for the shower, I don't announce, "I'm going to sanctify myself." But that is exactly what I'm doing. The shower becomes that place where my physical body is sanctified. Cleansing the soul is a different matter, though. This is not something I can accomplish with a bar of soap. I must look to God. Only by His living water can I be cleansed on the inside. That's what sanctification is. It's the process by which the Lord washes us from within.

Now let's talk about consecration. This is an act of *devotion*. Let's go back to the shower to understand what this means. Again, it is in the shower where I cleanse my body of all filth. But there must be some level of devotion on my part. I must devote myself to this process each day, lest I stinketh unto high heaven. Yes, it is up to me to strip myself of all things material before entering into that place of cleansing. The same is true if we are to be thoroughly washed within. We step out of the flesh then enter into that place where God can get his Hands on us. He, in turn, scrubs us up and washes away all the filth. In summary, sanctification means *cleanse* while consecration is an act of devotion. Sanctification is God business, consecration falls into our court. But one doesn't happen without the other. You might think of it as a divine transaction. We give God our devotion, He gives us a good washing. It's a swap where we come out on top!

Chapter 16
Thy People

"For wherein shall it be known here that I and thy people have found grace in thy sight? Is it not in that thou goest with us?" (Exodus 33:16)

Let's ask the very question Moses proposed. I'll phrase it in simpler terms: *how might the world know we have found grace in God's sight?* Will there be a visible trail? If your footsteps were to be followed, would any trace of grace be found? Generally speaking, God is not hard to track. He leaves behind a trail of goodness. If He truly goes with you, His grace will surely follow. There will be blessings you can point to, opened doors and joys to be told of. His peace, joy and wisdom will bear testimony to all – *the Lord is with you!* Perhaps you've noticed this in others who walk with God. There is something about them: a gentle spirit, a joyful countenance, a peace that surpasses all understanding. Let's face it, when the Lord goes with you, it shows -- your nature reflects His. But as we have already established, God does not go everywhere we go. He is not a follower. He only goes with those who follow Him. If we truly desire others to see that we have found grace in God's sight, we must follow His lead. His grace is sure to follow as we do.

Moses wasn't searching for answers when he proposed his question. No, there was much more to it than that. He was planting a seed. In his own tactful way, Moses was reminding the Lord (not that He had forgotten) that the Israelites were "thy people." And perhaps God's humble servant was reminding himself of this fact as well. It is quite liberating when ministers come to realize that the people they serve are "Thy people" and not "my people." The weight of trying to change others is immediately lifted and the minister becomes less of a control freak. The one who refers to his flock as "my people" runs himself ragged trying to micro-manage everyone. He learns very quickly that this is extremely exhausting and is best left to the Holy Spirit. I'm pretty sure Moses breathed a huge sigh of relief when he uttered those two words - *thy people*. Moses further reminded God that unless He joined them on their journey, no one would ever know that the Israelites were His people. Moses must have feared how this might look in the eyes of nations that trusted foreign gods.

Finally, there was an underlying petition in Moses' question. It's as if he were saying, "Lord, you have to do something about Thy people!" For Moses knew that not all his chums back at camp were in good graces with their God. The distance was still great and the Israelites lacked the wherewithal to rectify the situation. There was only one solution as far as Moses could see – the grace of God. Moses was keenly aware that the stiff-necked Israelites were not worthy of one fraction of the Lord's presence. Eternal separation is what they deserved. If there was to be any reconciliation at all, God would have to reach out on the basis of grace alone. And solely on that premise, the Lord purposed to draw near to His people.

As of yet we have not seen sanctification. Nor do we see consecration. There has been no cleansing from above and there is zero devotion below. All we observe at this point is determination on the Lord's part. He makes the first move. This is how it always is. You see, before sanctification or consecration can take place, something else must happen. There must first be conviction. Conviction can only occur when God comes near. Obviously, Moses realized this. He understood that the people of Israel would remain estranged, unless God Himself convicted them of their sin personally. Now, we have seen some positive steps on behalf of the Israelites. They did grieve over the loss of God's presence. They have been quite courteous to wave at the Lord from their tent doors. However, they have failed to deal with any walls of separation. They have yet to be broken. There is no clear indication of Godly sorrow. Aaron had his sorry excuses for the golden calf; no doubt everyone else had theirs as well. *"Yeah it was a mistake but..."* Unless God comes near, man will continue to rationalize sin. That's just our nature. But we run out of excuses once God shows up. His very presence brings conviction.

Perhaps you are one who can easily identify with the Israelites at this stage. You find yourself in a similar place. You grieve over the loss of God's presence. You readily recognize that you are not as close to Him as you once were. Maybe you can even pinpoint the sin causing this distance. But as of yet, there has been no real conviction. Instead of Godly sorrow, there has just been one rationalization after another for why you do what you do. I appeal to you, allow your heart to be convicted by His Spirit. Permit yourself to be humbled by His presence. Recommit your life to the Lord and He will wash you white as snow. Furthermore, He will go with you... and His grace will surely follow!

Chapter 17
We Shall Be Separate

*"So shall we be separated, I and thy people, from
all the people that are
upon the face of the earth"* (Exodus 33:16).

There are all kinds of people in the world. While many
blend in with the crowd, others stand out as unique. Take
the genres of music for example. Mention "punk rocker"
and a certain persona will come to mind. The same is true
with respect to rappers, metal-heads and country western
singers. One wears baggy jeans, the other wears torn jeans
while the other wears Wranglers. Hairstyle and hats might
also identify with a particular group. However, these things
reveal little about the soul. They don't help to identify the
child of God. Christians come in all shapes, sizes and fla-
vors. Some wear cowboy hats, others wear ball caps and
some prefer do-rags. One enjoys hip-hop, while another is
into bluegrass. So, what sets the child of God apart? Is it
the person on the outside or the inside?

When Moses declared, *"So shall we be separated,"* he was by no means trying to be exclusive. Nor was he suggesting that the Israelites were a notch above the rest and would therefore avoid any contact with the inferior commoners of the world. Moses' statement had nothing to do with group affiliation, ethnic pride or nationalism. His words get a little muddled for some in the English language. What Moses meant was, "We shall be a distinguished people." Indeed, if the Israelites possessed the very presence of God, they would be notably different from those who did not. The same goes for you and me, fellow Christian. If God is truly with us, we won't resemble the world. We will walk in the spirit, not in the flesh as others do. On a grander level, a God-fearing nation shows no resemblance to a God-rejecting nation. They are poles apart, as light is to darkness. Jesus had much to say about light and darkness. Here are just a few examples:

> *"And this is the condemnation, that light is come into the world, and men loved darkness rather than light, because their deeds were evil"* (John 3:19).

> *"Then spake Jesus again unto them, saying, I am the light of the world: he that followeth me shall not walk in darkness, but shall have the light of life"* (John 8:12).

> *"I am come a light into the world, that whosoever believeth on me should not abide in darkness"* (John 12:46).

Without question, Jesus was different. He stood out. He shined! If He is with us, we will too. We will reflect His glorious light. That light may make others uncomfortable. There are those who will run from it. Just as roaches scatter when the light comes on, there are people who do the same. The fact is, many favor darkness over light. They don't want to be exposed, so they quickly run for cover. Maybe there were a few who left your company rather upset because the light shined too brightly. Before stomping off, they might have snapped, "I'm tired of being judged by you!" The reality is you never spoke a single word that could have ever provoked such an accusation. No, the condemnation didn't come from you; they just couldn't handle the light. Though there are many who run from the light, there are also those who are quite drawn to it. They recognize it for what it is -- God's very presence! And that's exactly what they long for!

Once we embrace God's presence, His glorious light shines from within. Yes, we are distinctly unique in that respect. We walk differently. We talk differently. We even think and reason differently. The hairstyle remains the same and the jeans remain the same, but there is something inside that sets us apart. That something is God's light. This does not make us superior to others. It is merely the manifestation of a Supreme presence in our lives. It is not our own light shining, but a reflection of His magnificent light. Just as the moon reflects the sunlight, we mirror the light of God's Son. Paul explained it like this:

"For ye were sometimes darkness, but now are ye light in the Lord: walk as children of light: (For the fruit of the Spirit is in all goodness and righteousness and truth)" (Ephesians 5:8-9).

God's light always reflects *goodness and righteousness and truth.* We see these qualities in the life of Jesus. As we walk with Him, we will mirror these qualities as well. This is what distinguishes the child of God from the rest of the world. This is how we bear testimony to His presence. And this is what Moses had in mind when he declared, *"So shall we be separated... from all the people that are upon the face of the earth."*

We are to be a *distinguished* people, but we can easily become an *extinguished* people. Yes, there are things we can do to snuff out that divine light within. Jesus taught, *"No man, when he hath lighted a candle, putteth it in a secret place, neither under a bushel, but on a candlestick, that they which come in may see the light"* (Luke 11:33). When God sanctifies the believer, He clears out anything that might diffuse His light. The believer must continually consecrate himself so that God can have His way and so darkness won't creep back in. Unless a man consecrates himself, he is no different than the rest of the world. The light remains hidden. There is no evidence of a holy presence. God's desire is that others would be drawn to the light. You will know He is with you when that becomes your desire. The question we must ask at this point is, "What sets you apart from others?" Is it the outward man that identifies you with a particular group? Or is it the light within that identifies you with a particular Person? If it's the latter, let your light shine for all to see. It's the one and only thing that distinguishes us from a dark world.

Section X
Revelation

"For I neither received it of man, neither was I taught it, but by the revelation of Jesus Christ"
(Galatians 1:12).

Revelation: [Greek: apokalupsis] disclosure, appearing, manifestation.

Many years ago, I was out with some friends at a Denny's Restaurant. One of the guys in our company, Rick, was built like an army tank, standing six-foot-seven and weighing well over 300 pounds. He was all muscle and could knock a person out with the flick of his left pinky. Because it was rather late, we had the restaurant all to ourselves, with the exception of some youth on the other side of the partition. Though they were close by, we couldn't see each other clearly, only blurred silhouettes through textured glass. For some reason, these boys decided to razz us. However, a sudden hush fell upon them once my huge friend dropped by their table to introduce himself. This small gang of goofs received a personal revelation that demanded respect. Previously they had a foggy image of Rick. Upon his appearance, they knew him face to face and fear fell upon their very souls!

Indulge me to illustrate a revelation of a different sort. No doubt you must have seen "The Wizard of Oz." After one long, incredible journey, Dorothy and her skittish companions found themselves in the presence of the Great Oz himself. Initially, this wacky wizard was scarier than the wicked witch of the west. He appeared on the scene as an overblown face with a mean streak and a thunderous voice, which could shake the ears off an elephant. Dorothy's friends were initially intimidated by this inflated hot head. Their fears soon subsided once Toto offered a revelation of the true Oz. Once exposed, he was no longer someone to be feared. Oz was nothing more than a feeble dumpling who used low-tech media to overcome a little man complex. He probably never would have resorted to such tactics had he settled in Munchkin Land!

Revelation is a reality check. It unveils mysteries once hidden; the unknown becomes knowable. Why we need revelation from above is because it offers us a grander view of God. We see Him as He truly is and know that He is bigger than any of us could ever imagine. Revelation also helps us gain a better perspective of ourselves. We seem to shrink in the presence of the Almighty. We become less impressed with ourselves as our focus shifts to something higher, holier and more wonderful. Worship reaches new and exciting heights when a big God is seen through the eyes of a little man. We cannot help but to be in deeper awe of Him. We long to see Him magnified even more.

Chapter 18
The Glory of God

"And he said, I beseech thee, show me thy glory"
(Exodus 33:18).

Imagine a couple on their wedding night. Up until this point they have remained chaste. Now the two are alone in a five star honeymoon suite somewhere in the tropics. The wine has been poured, the lights have been dimmed, candles are flickering and piano music plays softly in the background. He looks at her longingly and says, "Show me thy glory!" It doesn't take a Rhode's scholar to read between the lines on that one. Obviously, the groom is looking forward to an unveiling of sorts. But there is more to it than just the shedding of clothes. He is declaring to his bride, *"I'm in total awe of you! I want to know your beauty as never before. I desire an encounter with you unlike any other. I long for an experience that I shall never share with anyone else save you."* A man such as this is not looking for cheap thrills where only he is gratified by the experience. This is one who seeks a higher appreciation for the one he loves.

I don't think it's a stretch to say Moses had similar feelings for God when he asked to see His glory. Don't misunderstand me, I don't mean this in a sensual way. Leave such thoughts for those who worship golden calves. But in the most pure sense, Moses desired deeper intimacy with his Lord. After all, he was caught up in the very presence of love divine. When you think about it, we do have all the key ingredients for the perfect romance novel -- Moses finds love, Moses and his love are separated, Moses pursues his love, the love of Moses returns and smothers him with affection… and hope… and peace… and promise. Call it what you will: captivated, enraptured or intoxicated. It was all that and more. Moses couldn't get enough! His passion for God was cranked into high gear. He longed to see God as he never saw Him before. He wanted to know His beauty like never before. He desired an encounter unlike any other. He sought to share an experience with God that would never be shared with another. This is how it is when we draw near to the Lord; our longing for Him becomes unquenchable. Once we stray, the opposite is true. We prefer distance. Not so when we draw near. The closer we get, the more of Him we crave. Moses was so close to God, he could almost touch Him. But it still wasn't near enough. "Show me thy glory!" he pleaded. It had to be said. A muzzle could not have silenced this man.

Deeper intimacy with the Lord can only lead to a heightened worship experience. I am convinced that is what Moses was after. There is no other reason why he'd request to see God's glory. He wasn't seeking an emotional lift; his desire was to lift up the Almighty. Isn't this the true heart of worship, to see Him lifted up? Worship never rises above our own individual perception of God. It remains proportionate to how we size Him up in our own eyes. When we don't see Him clearly, worship remains shallow.

As we zoom in, worship grows deeper. The closer we get, the bigger God becomes. As we drift away, He diminishes. There is a point to worship and it isn't so we can get a holy buzz. The objective is to draw as near to God as possible, so that He will be magnified, which simply means to make Him bigger.

Obviously, we cannot make God any bigger than He already is. It's silly to think we ever could. But the reality is that we can make God bigger! We can enlarge Him in our hearts and in our thoughts! We can magnify Him in our lives! And God can become really huge in our worship! A good way to start is to pray the words of Moses, "Show me thy glory!" Such a request is destined to revolutionize your Christian experience. And what about your Christian experience, my friend? Would you call it nominal or mediocre, at best? Perhaps you find yourself singing that old blues song, 'The Thrill is Gone.' I'm mindful of another blast from the past sung by Peggy Lee. Lamenting over life's many disappointments she croons, *"Is that all there is? If that's all there is, my friends, then let's keep dancing. Let's break out the booze and have a ball... if that's all there is."* In this sad ode the only thing magnified is a poor woman's pain. It is not my intent to sound unsympathetic. We all suffer disappointment, heartbreak and sorrows. No doubt Moses was in pain when Aaron and the rest of the camp checked out on God. And he was even more devastated when God checked out from the camp! But rather than see the man of woes magnified, he chose to see the God of wonders magnified. That's what we declare when we pray, "Show me thy glory!" We are saying, *"I'm done focusing on me. I only want to focus on You! I'm getting out of the way so I can see You as You truly are!"* Once we finally come to this place in our Christian experience, the honeymoon begins. God reveals Himself in exciting new ways!

Chapter 19
The Goodness of God

"And He said, I will make all my goodness pass before thee" (Exodus 33:19).

Three of the four gospel accounts describe how a rich, young ruler fell at the feet of Jesus asking, *"Good Teacher, what shall I do that I may inherit eternal life?"* (Mark 10:17) This curious nobleman was not complimenting our Lord's communication skills when he said "Good Teacher." He was acknowledging the goodness of His nature. Evidently the young dignitary had spent time observing Jesus. He saw first hand our Lord's compassion, grace and kindness. The story of the rich, young ruler follows immediately on the heels of Jesus receiving the children. The disciples wanted to run off these wee rascals, but Jesus quickly swept them up into His loving arms. No doubt, the young ruler was quite touched. When he finally meets up with Jesus, he goes face down. The curious fellow came with an important question. But he dared not ask it without a proper tribute to Jesus' goodness. Interestingly enough, the young ruler found his kind words challenged as if he might have missed a deeper truth to them. *"Why callest thou me good?"* Jesus implored. *"There is none good but one, that is, God"* (Mark 10:18). The intent of our Lord's probing was to get this young man to think his remark through. If Jesus is good (should we follow His logic), it can only be because He is God! On the other hand, if Jesus is merely a man, then He can't rightly be called "good" for all have sinned and fall short of God's glory.[1]

As the conversation ensued the young ruler was prompted to evaluate his own (self perceived) goodness. *"Thou knowest the commandments,"* said Jesus *"Do not commit adultery, Do not kill, Do not steal, Do not bear false witness, Defraud not, Honor thy father and mother."*[2] Reciting these laws was Jesus' way of holding a mirror for his newfound friend to look into. Most of us don't like mirrors because they tell the truth. They reveal every spot, blemish, bag, sag and wrinkle. We might think we're full of glory, but the mirror tells another story. That's the purpose of the law. It points out every flaw then points us to the fix. Sadly, when the young ruler looked into the mirror, he was quite impressed with what he saw. His chest must have been puffed out like a proud peacock when he declared, *"Master, all these have I observed from my youth."*[3] Though this "good" fellow managed to impress the apostles who stood nearby, his exalted opinion of self was not shared by Jesus. It was quickly pointed out where this self-made man lacked. The true test of his goodness came when he was asked to leave his material world behind and follow after the Lord. Unfortunately, he bailed in the opposite direction. This story shows us that man's goodness falls way

---

[1] Romans 3:23
[2] Mark 10:19
[3] Mark 10:20

short. In the presence of Jesus you would think a person might get that!

When the first man and woman were created they were endowed with goodness. The Genesis account notes that all things God created were good: the light, the sky, the land and waters. It was all good; and so were all the wonderful creatures that filled the earth. Yet mankind possessed a goodness that could not be matched by any other creature. How is that? We were created in God's likeness! Once God breathed His Spirit of life into that first couple. They were endued with goodness from on high. It was at the forbidden tree where the apple of death took a bite out of Adam and Eve. The compromising couple was emptied of that divine goodness they each possessed and they immediately felt naked without it. Sin left them and all of humanity empty, exposed, defiled and disconnected from the Father.

Fast forward now to the cross at Calvary. It is here where Jesus made it possible for us to reclaim the goodness of God. In John 20 we find the resurrected Christ breathing life back into mankind: *"He breathed on them, and said to them, 'Receive the Holy Spirit'"* (20:22). This is the promise for all who place their faith in Christ Jesus; He breathes His Spirit back into us. As a result, our own spirit awakens from the dead. Yes, we once again become living vessels of God's goodness. This is what it means to be born again. First we are born of the water (which represents physical birth) then we must be born of the spirit.[1]

Moses lived in a post-fall/pre-cross era. True (godly) goodness did not dwell in the heart of sinful man in those days. Such goodness could be found in God alone. Yet Moses understood what the hope of the "Promised Land" held. It served as the backdrop for the "Promised One," who would restore goodness into mankind once again. This was for another time and another generation. Realizing this,

---

[1] John 3

Moses sought desperately to capture a glimpse of coming attractions. Happy to oblige, God allowed His goodness to pass before him. Some feel bad for Moses because he never did enter into the Land flowing with milk and honey. Personally, I think he got the better end of the deal. We seldom consider the fact that he entered into something far more glorious than the Promised Land. Knowing Moses, he would have gladly traded all the milk and honey in the world for what he experienced. What about you, would you pass up an opportunity like this? Would you trade everything you have for a momentary encounter with God's goodness? Until we come to that place, God's glory will continually be eclipsed by our own.

> *"Then I will give them one heart, and I will put a new spirit within them, and take the stony heart out of their flesh, and give them a heart of flesh, that they may walk in My statutes and keep My judgments and do them; and they shall be My people, and I will be their God"* (Ezekiel 11:19-20).

Chapter 20
The Name of God

"... and I will proclaim the name of the LORD before thee"
(Exodus 33:19).

Some names warm our hearts. Others make us cringe. For example, any reference to names like Billy Graham or Mother Teresa is bound to win an approving nod. That's because these people are typically associated with goodness. However, the mere mention of Adolph Hitler or Osama bin Laden will surely solicit scowls among the noble. These names are not generally associated with goodness, at least in the home of the free and the brave. We can make similar observations with brand names. After some major blow-outs on a line of tires fitted for Ford Explorers, Firestone earned a blemish on an otherwise respectable name. A recall was quickly issued and 2000 proved to be a "good year" for "Goodyear'," who replaced the bulk of these dreaded treads. Firestone has made great strides in redeeming their name, and most have forgotten the infamous recall that cost this major corporation gazillions. But for those who owned Ford Explorers at the time of this legendary rubber-flub, they may not be so forgiving should Firestone be recommended for tire replacements.

Names are more than just labels. We associate them with quality, integrity and reputation -- or the lack thereof. We think in terms of character or character flaws: goodness versus wickedness, bravery versus cowardice, ingenuity versus futility, the list goes on and on. To illustrate, what comes to mind when you hear the name Michael Jackson? Does it creep you out? Or does it make you wish you were under a disco ball dancing to *Billy Jean*? Let's try another, how about O.J. Simpson? Are you thinking football? Or are you haunted by a senseless and brutal murder? There are others we could throw in the mix that might raise an eyebrow or two: Bill Clinton, Martha Stewart or Jerry Falwell. We think of what these people represent, their values and the quality of their character. We think of their successes as well as their failures. For some odd reason I will always associate the name Geraldo Rivera with Al Capone's vault. I realize it was decades ago when he televised himself opening up that barren box but I haven't let it go. To me Geraldo will always be the sensationalist who invades primetime programming for a close up shot of, well... nothing! Let's face it -- there is more behind a name than just a string of letters. Our entire reputation is wrapped up in these little tags.

Now I must ask, what comes to mind when you hear the name of the Lord? Does it comfort you? Bless you? Encourage you? Does it drop you to your knees? Do your eyes to twinkle or tear up? Do your lips tremble or sing? There was obvious rejoicing when David wrote, *"I will praise the LORD according to his righteousness: and will sing praise to the name of the LORD most high."*[1] Elsewhere the

---

[1] Psalm 7:17

psalmist declared, *"Blessed be the name of the LORD from this time forth and forevermore."[1]* David invited others to honor the name above all names when he penned, *"Let them praise the name of the LORD: for his name alone is excellent; his glory is above the earth and heaven."[2]* David's son, Solomon, also had a high regard for the name of the Lord as we see in the following proverb, *"The name of the LORD is a strong tower: the righteous runneth into it, and is safe."[3]* Then there was poor Job. Even in the direst of straits he would declare, *"The LORD gave, and the LORD hath taken away; blessed be the name of the LORD"* (Job 1:21).

What makes *the Name* is *the One* who possesses it: His character, His divine nature, His holiness. The name of the Lord represents goodness, greatness and graciousness. It speaks of forgiveness, deliverance and salvation; righteousness and truth. It's packed with power, might and authority -- all that wonderfully wrapped in abounding love, endless mercy and gentle compassion. The name of the Lord is to be adored, revered and trusted. It is a name to be both celebrated and feared. We cheerfully shout it from the mountaintop and we tearfully cry it from the valley. There is no other like it. Holy is His name!

It is interesting that the name of the Lord is never fully spelled out in original manuscripts of the Old Testament. He is often called God, but that is not His name, that's simply who He is. As a matter of a fact, the Lord is called many things in the Bible: Father, Creator, Almighty, the list goes on. It was at the burning bush when Moses finally popped God for some ID, but all He would say was, *"I AM that I AM"*.[4] Some say His name is pronounced Jehovah, while others insist that it's Yahweh. We don't really know

---

[1] Psalm 113:2
[2] Psalm 148:13
[3] Proverbs 18:10
[4] Exodus 3:14

for sure. All the ancient scribes offer are a few consonants without the benefit of any vowels. Not even Pat Sajak or Vanna White can help us with this one. As far as we can tell from the Old Testament, the name of the Lord is shrouded in mystery. Though a tight lid was kept on the Name above all names, the prophets of old did offer this wonderful promise, *"And it shall come to pass, that whosoever shall call on the name of the LORD shall be delivered"* (Joel 2:32). This promise would be fulfilled in the New Testament where we are finally given the name of the Lord: *"But ye are justified in **the name of the Lord Jesus**, and by the Spirit of our God"* (1 Corinthians 6:11). (Bold print mine.)

And now we have a name, a personal name – Jesus! It is a name that holds promise and delivers the moment it is embraced. Literally, Jesus means "God is salvation." There is no other name in our vast universe that breathes such hope. The apostle Peter put it this way, *"Neither is there salvation in any other: for there is none other name under heaven given among men, whereby we must be saved"* (Acts 4:12). Yes, it is a name we can call upon. It is the name by which we are saved. It is the name by which we can know God as a friend. The mere fact that God can now be known by name is evidence enough that He desires a personal relationship with each and every one of us. Twice in Exodus 33 the Lord tells Moses, "I know you by name." But Moses, as of yet, did not know God by His name. He only knew Him as the great "I AM," The prayer of Moses changed all that. He would know God like never before. He would know Him more intimately. He would know Him by name. Like Moses, we too have a name we can connect with. It is the name proclaimed from on high, the Name above all names: Jesus! Through this wonderful name we can know God like never before.

*"Blessed be the King that cometh in the name of the Lord:
peace in heaven,
and glory in the highest"* (Luke 19:38).

*"But these are written that you may believe
that Jesus is the Christ, the Son of God,
and that believing you may have life in His
name"* (John 20:31).

Chapter 21
The Nature of God

"And [I] will be gracious to whom I will be gracious, and will show mercy on whom I will show mercy" (Exodus 33:19).

It is amazing how believers and unbelievers view things so differently. Tell an unbeliever of God's grace and mercy, he's all smiles. To quickly kill the conversation, speak of God's righteousness and how He judges sin. Christians, on the other hand, appear to have embraced the idea of a just God. "Vengeance is mine!" says the Lord, and as far as we're concerned, He can take it and run with it. Judgment and the punishment of evil only seem fair. The thing that gets under our skin is grace and mercy. We rather like being on the receiving end of it, mind you. But we prefer that God didn't extend these favors to people we don't like. While the Lord would prefer to see us lighten up, there are times we want to see Him tighten up. He's far too liberal when it comes to dishing out grace and mercy! There should be stricter criteria when it comes to qualifying for these heavenly perks. Even then, grace and mercy should be divvied out sparingly. It's that conservative nature of ours. We can't help but wonder whether the reserve on these commodities is running low. We want to make sure there is enough to cover our backsides. As far as justice is concerned, God can be as generous as He likes with that stuff. Let's hope there's enough to go around for everyone! That is… *everyone but us!*

Several years ago, actress Jane Fonda professed to have converted to Christianity. This greatly upset one particular Vietnam veteran I know. He did not think it fair of God to save someone who marched to the beat of an "anti-American" drum, even if it was almost four decades ago. He is not alone. There are extremists who believe fire and brimstone are the appropriate response to anyone not voting Republican! Personally, I'm good with a nonpartisan God. My pet peeve is fallen preachers, those who have disgraced the pulpit with their philandering or fraudulence. I could even name a few, and should I do so the last thing I want to hear is – *"the Lord will be gracious to whom He will be gracious, and will show mercy on whom He will show mercy."* Honestly, I'd rather make that call. And I'm sure you have your own "top 10" list. Maybe there are some real dirt-bags on it like: Tex Watson of the Manson family, the Son of Sam or Ted Bundy, all murderers who have since professed faith in Jesus Christ. I think we'd all prefer a vote of hands than leave it up to God to decide the fate of these so called "creeps." That's because we each know exactly how He tends to lean… grace and mercy every time. He's simply too generous with such things. It isn't fair, is it?

As unfair as we may think God is, we do seem to identify with that one "lucky" thief who was crucified next to Jesus. For good reason, too! We invariably put ourselves in his place. It's a wonderful proposition to be promised paradise without having past sins taken into account. We don't mind at all swapping places with that wretched fellow, do we? But tag someone else's name on the rascal and we have to think things through a little more thoroughly. "Wait a minute!" we object, "That crook was bad to the bone! Make him pay! Where's the justice?" You won't get any argument out of me. I'm on the same page. That thief was rotten to the core; he deserved to be punished to the full extent of the law. By no means did he deserve one ounce of grace or even the tiniest smidgen of mercy. But then... *who does?*

Perhaps you've heard the following illustration of God's grace: a criminal stands before a judge and is declared guilty of his offense. He is sentenced to life in prison but, lo and behold, Mr. Bleeding-heart pops out of nowhere and offers to do his time for him. This touching anecdote has been a favorite among Sunday school teachers to explain how Jesus stepped in for us when we were found guilty. Cute story -- but it's not even close to the real deal! Let's go back to the courtroom for a more accurate picture: a criminal is convicted of every crime in the book. He receives multiple life sentences for his numerous offenses. The judge sets down his gavel and _he_ offers to do the time for Mr. Bad-guy. We're not done yet, hold on... Next, the judge hands the convict a set of keys saying, "This one is for my mansion, this one is for my Lexus and the third is for my safety deposit box where I stash all the cash. It's all yours now. Enjoy!" With all due respect, I believe this illustration paints a more accurate picture of what Jesus did on our behalf. He is the one who pardons and pays for our sin. That's what we call "mercy." Next we are given the keys to paradise. We call that "grace." Mercy is when God withholds what we deserve – we deserve to be on death row! Grace is God giving us what we do not deserve – eternal life in heaven.

We will never fully understand it, but God does not deal with us based on what we deserve or what we may think we deserve. He relates to His children on the basis of mercy and grace. For whatever reason, this was his message to Israel's leader. It remains somewhat of a mystery to me why God chose this particular moment to tell Moses, *"And I will be gracious to whom I will be gracious, and will show mercy on whom I will show mercy."* But then, sometimes it's better to focus on the practical than venture off into the mystical where lessons are oftentimes lost. In light of what Moses prayed, I think the Lord's response was more than appropriate. As righteous as he was, Moses was not entitled to anything. Nor is God ever under any obligation to anyone. We need to understand this when we approach Him, He owes us nothing. We are in no position to make demands of God. There is not one thing we can ask for which we are deserving of. When we come to Him, we can only appeal to His mercy and grace. Answered prayer is simply God being nice. That is why we seek Him diligently. Not because we are nice. Not because we are worthy. But because He is!

Chapter 22
The Face of God

"But He said, "You cannot see My face; for no man shall see Me, and live" (Exodus 33:20).

As we have already learned from the previous chapter, when God gives us what we ask for it can only be attributed to His amazing grace. Then there are those occasions when prayer goes unanswered, at least according to our expectations. Whether we wish to accept it or not, the Lord intentionally withholds from us from time to time. Not to deprive us, but to spare us. When He holds back, it's typically an act of mercy. Being the wise One that He is, God knows what we can handle. He also knows what we *cannot* handle! I suppose in this respect, our Heavenly Father is like many other concerned fathers. He's not going to act willy-nilly by giving His children everything they ask for. I know I don't operate that way. If my daughter asks for something that could potentially harm her, I will withhold that thing. It might not even be a bad thing. She's just not in a place in her life where she can handle it. Or maybe she can handle a little, but not a lot. I might be a bit nervous about handing my 16-year-old ten-grand in cold cash but I might go as high as a hundred! (Mind you, I said *"might"*.) But even a hundred bucks is an act of grace on my part. Not giving her the full wad is mercy. It's not that I want to deprive her; I'd rather set it aside for a time when she's better equipped to handle that much loot.

The more I ponder this, the more I am convinced that God was introducing His divine policy for answering prayer when He said, *"And I will be gracious to whom I will be gracious, and will show mercy on whom I will show mercy."* Don't get me wrong, I believe this statement covers a lot more territory than just prayer. But God does seem to act on this principle when it comes to complying with Moses' request to see His glory. It's as if the Lord were telling Moses, "If I do, it's because I'm gracious. If I don't, it's because I'm merciful." We certainly can't fault Moses for wanting an eyeful of glory, but the Lord would only meet him part way. He had no other choice. You see, God's glory outshines the sun. As beneficial as the sun is to life on our planet, Gold holds back on that, too. If it were any closer we'd all be toast; if it were any further we'd be popsicles. The good Lord placed this magnificent fireball where it could be appreciated from a safe distance. We can marvel at the sun's splendor as it rises upon the mountains or sets upon the sea. But you still wouldn't want to stare it in the face in its brightest hour. The same is true with God's glory. No man can look God in the face and survive the experience. It's more glory than our fallen nature can handle.

Some might think Moses was a little presumptuous in asking to see God's glory. Personally, I think such boldness shows maturity on his part. There was a time when all Moses could do was look away from the Lord. Consider that frightful encounter at the burning bush: *"And Moses hid his face; for he was afraid to look upon God."* (See Exodus 3:6.) Thirty chapters later this same shaken shepherd seems to have overcome his fears. What's changed? Their relationship! Moses now knows God on a more personal level. He knows His nature. He knows His way. These two are friends, whereas before, God was the mysterious arsonist who spoke from a flaming shrub. Also, I think Moses must have sensed how much he pleased the Father by seeking His presence. This humble leader could stand before the Lord unashamed. What about you? Will such be the case when Jesus returns in all His glory? I fear He will be a stranger to countless professed Christians. They will look away once He shows up. However, a few will welcome their friend as though they were expecting Him. They will gaze upon His face and marvel at His glory. It all comes down to where we are at with Him presently. If we are found seeking the Lord when He comes, naturally we will want to gaze upon Him when He is revealed in the clouds. But if we are not waiting upon His return, we might be inclined to turn away. This isn't rocket science. It's simple, common sense. We all know it deep down. It's just a matter of whether we care or not. And isn't that the mark of true friendship? Yes, friends care! Should it come to light that we don't, we'll have good reason to turn away once God's glory appears in the clouds. That wasn't the case with Moses. He had a heart for God. And God had a heart for him! And lest He give Moses a heart attack, God chose to hide His face from the curious fellow.

I have one more thing to say on this matter before we move to our next topic. I do not believe the reports of those who claim to have seen God and, based upon the passage we just considered, neither should you. The Apostle John also affirms, *"No man hath seen God at any time."*[1] While scripture states this as fact, there are popular televangelists

---

[1] John 1:18

who have convinced their viewers otherwise. I'm mindful of one particular preacher on "Christian cable" who boasts of close encounters of the most absurd kind. I must admit he is quite charming and amusing to listen to, but his claims are too far fetched for anyone who would dare open the Bible. If we are to believe this notorious dreamer, he is among the privileged few who have actually spent quality time with God in heaven. While there, he had the good fortune of watching the great I AM produce baby angels. They just seemed to pop out of his mouth every time He exhaled. The interesting thing about his account is that he speaks of his heavenly trip as if it were a visit to Starbucks. It's as if he sees this kind of stuff all the time. There is no sense of awe or wonder as he retells his story. You might even think that the Lord's presence left him unimpressed or that the glory of God was no more spectacular than that of a bottle rocket. When you hear these tall tales you know somebody is lying. You must decide whether it is the one who claims to have seen God, or God who claims in His Word that no man has ever seen Him. The follow up question would be – if that person really did see the face of God, how is it that he lived to tell about it?

A transformation must occur before fallen man can gaze into the eyes of God. Either God must transform and take on a flesh nature like ours, which He did 2000 years ago in the person of Jesus Christ. Or, we must take on a glorified nature like His. This will occur when we shed our flesh and pass from this life to the next. Until that happens, we just get snapshots of God's glory. You may wish to call them 'previews of coming attractions'. The apostle Paul expressed it this way, *"For now we see through a glass, darkly; but then face to face: now I know in part; but then shall I know even as also I am known"* (1 Corinthians 13:12). Though things may appear a little fuzzy right now, there is still enough glory to marvel at. And it will only get better!

Section XI
Reconciliation

"For if, when we were enemies, we were recon-
ciled to God by the death of his Son, much more,
being reconciled, we shall be saved by his life"
(Romans 5:10).

Reconcile: [Greek, *katallasso*] to change mutually

As I write, intelligible words are being processed into
my laptop. Once this manuscript is put into book form, you
will know that it finally made it to a printer. A laptop and a
printer are not anything alike. A laptop is a master. A
printer is a slave which follows orders. Before a laptop can
communicate orders to a printer, a connection must be
made. There must be some sort of interface which under-
stands both computers and printers. Next, some necessary
conversions must take place. Print drivers and software
programs will aid in reconciling these two devices so that

they become compatible with each other. Then they can talk.

God and man are also very different. While it is true we are created in His image, that likeness was greatly compromised after the fall. He is holy, we are not. He is righteous, we are not. He is sinless, we are not. Because of these things, a compatibility problem exists between God and man. For imperfect man to be joined to a perfect God, a connection must be made. Something must come between us to serve as an interface. That something must have both "God" qualities and "man" qualities. Only Jesus fits this description. Being fully God and at the same time fully man, He can connect humanity with divinity. We are not finished, yet. A conversion must also take place. The process of reconciliation denotes mutual change. In other words, a conversion must take place on each end. God must change to be compatible with man. Man must change to be compatible with God. Reconciliation can't work any other way. Unless there is change on both sides, true reconciliation has not taken place. God was the first to initiate change. Two thousand years ago He took on a nature of flesh. The Apostle John explains it like this:

"And the Word was made flesh, and dwelt among us, (and we beheld his glory, the glory as of the only begotten of the Father,) full of grace and truth" (John 1:14).

We must accept this testimony for change to occur within us. Once we believe, a conversion immediately takes place on our end. Our spirit comes alive. Furthermore, God's Spirit takes up residence with ours. Now we can talk. There is connection, conversion and, finally, communication.

Chapter 23
A Place by Me

"And the LORD said, Behold, there is a place by me"
(Exodus 33:21a).

I suspect many believe there truly is a place beside God. Some do wonder, though, how to get there or, perhaps, whether they can get there at all. What about you, are you curious about such a place? Do thoughts like these boggle your mind: Is it a tangible place? A geographical place? Is it Jerusalem or maybe Mecca? How about the Vatican? Perhaps that place is a holy hill somewhere, or an altar or a shrine! Does God provide a map to that place by Him? We should check the back of our Bibles at once... Maybe the fifth missionary journey of Paul will lead us there... Or maybe it's a heavenly place beyond our reach! If there is such a place, it would also be helpful to know whether it's occupied or not. Will there be a big sign posted that reads "no vacancy" or "off limits" or "no trespassing" or "take a number?" Do you think there will be a long line to that place, like the one at the mall where runny nose kids wait to sit on Santa's lap at Christmastime?

It is a peculiar thing to me that God would offer Moses a place by Him. After all, they were already behaving as dear chums and chatting face to face. From my perspective, it hardly seems possible that a person could have gotten any nearer to the Lord. But that's just how it is, the longer we linger in His presence the nearer to Him we are drawn. No matter how near you are to the Lord, there is always room to move in a little closer, there is always some distance to leave behind. In this divine romance we find ourselves on a never ending quest to eliminate as much space as possible between us and the One whom we seek. That is where the journey begins – in seeking Him. From that point on, God takes it from there. He clears the way. He makes room. He brings us to that sacred place few dare to visit. It is a marvelous vista point where we capture the ultimate view of God's glory. You won't see it all there, but it's more than you'll ever catch this side of heaven.

There are many places near God. It may be a prayer closet or a back porch. It could be on a private beach or a quiet spot in the woods. Wherever the Lord is sought, there is found a place by Him. For those who do not seek Him, that place remains foreign. It is unexplored territory. The frontier of the complacent remains a spiritual wasteland. The stagnant soul can never know the beauty of that place near God. What about you? Have you found your place by God? If so, I submit there is a place even closer, one even more glorious. And once you've discovered that place, there is another closer still. The Christian journey is filled with places by God. Each one prepares us for the next. Each one gets us nearer and nearer to the Lord. For Moses, the Tabernacle of Meeting was a place near God. The divine romance took to greater depths in that humble tent. Yet in the big scheme of things, that place was just a starting point. God drew Him closer still. The same is true for each of us. We will never find that perfect place where we just can't draw any nearer to God. He's forever nudging us closer. He is forever carrying us over the next threshold to that sweeter place by Him. The invitation "come" echoes out into the distance. Nearness does not seem to ever silence it. It rings louder upon every approach. The only thing that seems to muffle God's voice is the whine of our own when we say, "I'm fine where I'm at." It is the claim of every sluggard who proudly stands upon a distant and slippery slope!

Such is the life of a sojourner, we venture from place to place. The rest God offers will never be found in idleness. Rest is not found in one place but in a series of places. He lifts us higher that we might grow deeper. He takes us further that we might grow closer. There is nothing more detrimental to the Christian faith than stagnancy. It is the leading cause of spiritual lethargy. It is a trap we must avoid. We can only be still long enough to hear God speak. He keeps us on the move. We are continually advancing forward, lest the journey end. There is that kind and gentle voice which whispers into our hearts, "Your time here is finished. Get moving." We are never pushed, only prompted. Yes, we may so choose to linger in a solitary spot. We might even grow comfortable there. But God's glory moves on. You will quickly lose sight of it should you dig your heels too deep. Our options must be carefully weighed; we can linger in one place or we can follow God's trail. Those who seek his glory never retire. We do not settle at any one spot. The journey of the soul never ends. It's always on the move, seeking, yearning for that next place nearer to God.

Moses experienced a wonderful encounter with God in that sacred tent he pitched outside the camp. Had he lingered too long, though, he would have lost sight of His glory. The Lord had arranged for a view more intimate, more spectacular. Moses eventually had to venture out from that holy tabernacle. Had he not journeyed on, God's glory would have faded before his eyes. It's like taking in the Grand Canyon. You can enjoy it from a bird's eye view out of the window of an airplane. Or you can explore its depths by entering into it. But the plane must land. You must step out and journey into the canyon. Before long, you will be surrounded by all the splendors the Canyon has to offer. Likewise, Moses had to step out from his tent. He was then brought to a place where he was surrounded by glory divine. He was placed in the cleft of a rock. But he didn't overstay his welcome there, either. The Lord moved him on. And so it goes with each of us.

If there is that longing to be near God, a yearning to see His glory, you must fight idleness as if it were your fiercest foe. No one place remains sacred for too long. God's presence does not rest on our merry plateaus. Once His glory moves on the adversary quickly moves in, bidding us to stay put. Keep moving, my friend! Move from glory to glory. Follow the voice of the One who leads you on to the next place -- that place by Him.

Chapter 24
The Rock

*"... and thou shalt stand upon a rock: And it shall
come to pass, while my glory passeth by, that I
will put thee in a cleft of the rock, and will cover
thee with my hand while I pass by: And I will take
away mine hand, and thou shalt see my back
parts: but my face shall not be seen"*
(Exodus 33:21b-23).

With all due respect, Moses was not some superhero
with superpowers. The only thing that kept him from bowing before the golden calf was – he was in the right place at
the right time. God could have called anyone up the mountain. Had He asked for a show of hands, there would have
been plenty of volunteers ready to make the ascent. And
they, too, would have squeaked out of the whole cow mess.
But the Lord called Moses. Otherwise, there is no telling
what this man may have done if stuck below with all those
grumblers pacing at the foothills. We just don't know

which way he might have swayed had he been caught up in all the huffing and hysteria.

The best we can say for Moses is -- the Lord led him not into temptation and delivered him from all evil. But lack of opportunity does not prove the heart to be pure. To further illustrate, suppose a man is so unbecoming no gal will have him. He doesn't get points for that. He can still be an adulterer in his heart. We're sinners whether the opportunity is there or not. To quote Jeremiah, *"The heart is deceitful above all things, and desperately wicked: who can know it?"* (17:9)

What the prophet Jeremiah states is fact, without any exceptions. And if we can learn anything at all from the example of Moses it is this – the only thing that keeps us from sin is the very presence of God. Furthermore, if we're going to stand before a holy God, we need a covering!

Comparatively speaking, Moses did seem to be a notch above the rest. It does appear that, at least in this stage of his humble life, Moses had a true zeal for righteousness when most did not. He was making wise choices. He was a seeker. He was a worshipper. But that did not change the fact that Moses was a mortal being with a fallen nature. Dare I say of this legendary figure that he too was a sinner! He was a sinner with a passion for God. And he was a sinner who needed a covering. Regardless of how holy or heroic a person may be, we all need a covering when it comes to our dealings with God. Your pastor needs one, your priest needs one, Billy Graham needs one, you need one and I need one. As long as we remain in these corruptible bodies of flesh, we need a covering. Here is why: we cannot look fully upon God, nor can He look fully upon us. The result in either case would be fatal. We have already seen that no man can look upon God and live. The other aspect to this is -- if God were to look upon our flesh, He would have no other choice but to smoke us. Therefore, He covers us lest our sinful nature be exposed before Him.

When it comes right down to it, He covers us because He is merciful! Without a covering we'd all be toast!

Take special note of the provision made for Moses; it is a most curious thing. Firstly, the Lord stood him upon a rock. On that rock was a covering, a cleft. There this man of flesh remained hidden, safe and secure. From God's vantage point, He clearly saw the rock but not Moses. But God also provided a second covering, His hand. This was so Moses couldn't see God in all His consuming glory. He only saw what followed once His hand was removed, the afterglow, which was enough to knock Moses' socks off without taking his lights out. Yet even this vanishing trail of glory had our man lit up like the Fourth of July for days. The important thing to understand is this: even for a quick peek of God's backside, Moses required a covering. Without it, he'd have been a smoldering heap of ash.

What God has done for Moses, He has done for you and for me. Lest we be consumed in our sin, we are placed upon the rock. For us that rock is none other than Jesus Christ. There are numerous references to the divine rock throughout scripture. I'll quote just a few for you:

"He is the Rock, his work is perfect: for all his ways are judgment: a God of truth and without iniquity, just and right is he" (Deuteronomy 32:4).

"For in the time of trouble he shall hide me in his pavilion: in the secret of his tabernacle shall he hide me; he shall set me up upon a rock" (Psalm 27:5).

"And they remembered that God was their rock, and the high God their redeemer" (Psalm 78:35).

"Enter into the rock, and hide thee in the dust, for fear of the LORD, and for the glory of his majesty" (Isaiah 2:10).

"...for they drank of that spiritual Rock that followed them: and that Rock was Christ"
(1 Corinthians 10:4b).

So long as we stand upon this mighty Rock, all of our sins remain covered. We are sufficiently hidden in Christ Jesus. This is what separates the believer from the unbeliever. Neither is perfect, but one has a hiding place while the other does not. The sins of the unbeliever remain completely exposed while the sins of the believer are mysteriously and wonderfully covered. Unless we run for cover, our sins will be judged, a penalty will be paid. We find that the sins of the world were amply paid for at the cross. Should you reject this payment, the debt is charged to your account. Yes, you'll have to cover it. And the price is a hefty one! There's only one place to run for cover and only one person to turn to. We must stand upon the Rock. Once we are hidden in Christ, God no longer looks upon our iniquities. We are eternally secure in Jesus our Lord.

Furthermore, the hand of God goes with us. By His hand, He leads us from temptation and lovingly guides us into paths of righteousness. By His hand, He nudges us closer to Him. With His hand, He showers us with heavenly blessings. Like a skillful potter, He is shaping us into vessels of honor with His very own hand. By His hand, He provides everything we need. But most importantly of all, we are covered by the awesome hand of God. The reason is simple: we are not yet ready to look into the face of God. Though we may draw nearer to Him each day, He continues to cover us with His hand. We yearn for more of His glory, but He is only willing to grant what we can live to tell about. Tell of what you've seen thus far and soon you will discover more. The balance He will save until that blessed day when we are with Him. Until then, we keep our feet firmly planted upon the Rock.

"Thou art my hiding place; thou shalt preserve me from trouble; thou shalt compass me about with songs of deliverance" (Psalm 32:7).

Section XII
Proclamation

"… I will proclaim the name of the LORD before thee…"
(Exodus 33:19).

Proclaim: [Hebrew, qara] to call out to, cry, preach

Some folks have difficulty with the expression 'preach' as if it meant *nagging*. We might hear someone say, "Don't preach at me!" If we were to take them literally, they are actually saying, "Don't proclaim good news to me!" That's the true definition of preach, to proclaim good news: Quite frankly, I'm rather fond of the idea. You can preach at me anytime! And I certainly won't be insulted should you call me a preacher! To be a bearer of good news is an honor, and it's also a blast. All things considered, I'd rather be a preacher than a prophet. It seems prophets were usually the bearers of bad news. They generally warned idolaters and backsliders of impending wrath. They said things like, "Get it together or else!" Read Isaiah for example. There are some tasty nuggets in that book to be sure, but many of the verses would be frightening if you ever found them on a greeting card. They are not what we'd normally consider as inspirational. The same is true for Jeremiah. Then there was Jonah who told the Ninevites, "In 40 days you're all history!" Who wants that job? Not even Jonah wanted it. Ah, but to be a preacher! *"How beautiful upon the mountains are the feet of him that bringeth good tidings, that publisheth peace; that bringeth good tidings of good, that publisheth salvation; that saith unto Zion, Thy God reigneth!"* (Isaiah 52:7) I'll sign up for that job any ol' day! The business of preachers is to bring good tidings and to proclaim salvation. Ours is not a message of doom, but deliverance and hope. The good news we preach is Jesus Christ! Jesus saves! Preachers find themselves in excellent company. The original preacher was God Himself. The first time the word 'proclaim' is mentioned in the Bible is in Exodus 33:19 where God says, *"I will proclaim the name of the LORD before thee."* This announcement was first made millennia ago by the Most High. It has resonated unto every generation since then. It sounds forth even today. And the name of the Lord is still good news!

Chapter 25
God's User ID

"And the LORD descended in the cloud, and stood with him there, and proclaimed the name of the LORD" (Exodus 34:5).

It is not until the next verse (Exodus 34:6) that the Lord passes Moses in all his wondrous glory. But something significant happens just prior to that, something typically missed by even the most scrutinizing of Bible students. I cannot fault them for this; it's simply our tendency to miss things. We focus our eyes on the big picture and skip over details as if they were meant to be filed away into obscurity somewhere. Not just with scripture but with all kinds of stuff. Recently I purchased a Jeep Wrangler. I was so excited to find one with a hard top... and AC... and an automatic transmission! Most I looked at only scored two out of three, if that. After searching car dealerships on the internet from Austin to San Antonio, I finally found what I was looking for. The price was also right, so I paid a visit to the lot and drove her home. It wasn't until several days later that I discovered satellite radio on my tuner. It was an extra perk I just didn't expect. No doubt, I was thrilled! The Bible is like that as well. There are features we often miss. You can read the same account over and over again, and even though the big picture may not seem to change much, something fresh jumps out at you -- a nugget you never expected. I wonder if you might have missed what happened just prior to God revealing his glory to Moses. It's an exciting feature. Moses experiences something of unparalleled significance: *the Lord stood with Him!*

Why many tend to overlook this detail, I cannot explain for the life of me. Speaking from my own experience, I have heard numerous teachings on Moses' infamous encounter with God. I've also read several commentaries on the subject. However, both teachers and commentators alike seem to be silent with regard to how the Lord stood with Moses. I can't seem to let it go. I'd like to know why the Lord stood with him. And for how long! I do find it interesting that the Hebrew word used for "stood" also means "remained." Things like this make me curious. How long did God remain standing with Moses before showing off His glory? Five seconds? Five minutes? Five hours? Scripture doesn't tell us but my guess is – as long as necessary!

At this stage, God was still manifesting Himself in the form of a cloud. Although you and I might rank that as phenomenal, this was quite ordinary for Moses. As a matter of fact, every Israelite in the camp had been privy to seeing the Lord in this fashion. This is how He led them by day through the wilderness. The extraordinary thing here is not so much in how the Lord presents Himself, but that He actually stood with Moses. This is absolutely startling to me. It seems that God had but one purpose for standing with Moses. There was something He wanted him to get, something He didn't want to get lost in all the pizzazz. So God stood by Moses until it sunk deep into his thick noggin.

Moses was in for one incredible experience. He was about to have his mind blown. Soon the Lord would reveal His glory in ways no man had ever known before. But God made certain Moses wasn't blinded by the light. So, He stood with him awhile. And what did God do as He stood there? He preached! He proclaimed the name of the Lord. Signs, wonders and revelation are quite meaningless if the Name never sinks in. We can go to so called "revivals" and witness miracle upon miracle, or we can attend prophetic conferences and hear all kinds of amazing predictions. But if the Name is never proclaimed it's just smoke and mirrors. It may look or sound exciting, but it will have served no real purpose. It is never God's intention just to dazzle us. He has a much bigger agenda. He wants us to know Him for who He is. Visuals certainly help us to grasp God's glory, but they do little to help us connect with Him on an intimate level. We need a name to call upon.

This was to be an important lesson for Moses, and it should be for us as well. Faith is not the substance of things experienced or the evidence of things observed with the human eyeball. On the contrary, *"...faith is the substance of things hoped for, the evidence of things not seen"* (Hebrews 11:1). Therefore, we do not hang our hat on what we see. We hang it upon a name. Anything else, our experiences and so forth, are just flowers picked along the way. They may be beautiful to touch, smell or look upon, but they quickly fade. Faith will certainly fail us should it be placed in something that withers away or dissipates. Experiences don't last, they fade like a flower. Their beauty is but for a moment. So rather than give Moses a short-lived experience, God left him with something to hang onto, something of substance he could place his faith in, something he could share with others.

God could have very easily given Moses an experience and left it at that. Had He done so, Moses would have returned to the camp and told everyone about his amazing "experience." Naturally, everyone would have been talking about what Moses experienced and some would have wanted to seek a similar experience for themselves. But what happens when the glory of that experience fades? New experiences are sought. God didn't create us to be like rubber balls, bouncing from one phenomenon to the next. His deepest desire is that we would seek after Him. Therefore, He gives us a name.

> *"The name of the LORD is a strong tower: the righteous runneth into it, and is safe"* (Proverbs 18:10).

Chapter 26
God's Profile

"And the LORD passed by before him, and pro-
claimed, The LORD, The LORD God, merciful
and gracious, longsuffering, and abundant in
goodness and truth, Keeping mercy for thousands,
forgiving iniquity and transgression and sin, and
that will by no means clear the guilty; visiting the
iniquity of the fathers upon the children, and upon
the children's children, unto the third and to the
fourth generation" (Exodus 34:6-7).

You can look at me for as long as you may, but you will have learned very little about who I am on the inside. If you wish to know the man beneath the skin, we'll have to sit down and talk. Then I can share my story with you. Then you'll have a better idea about what makes me tick. The same is true with God. Obviously, we cannot learn about Him from looking at Him. We cannot see Him. But we can hear what He has to say. We can listen to His story. And by His Word we can know Him.

*　*　*　*　*

Visuals only reveal so much. Certainly, there is enough out there to convince any thinking person that there is a Supreme Designer who is responsible for everything that exists. So much so, there is no rational excuse for denying Him. All of creation bears testimony to a Creator. As we survey the world around us, we learn much about Him: He is intelligent, orderly, imaginative and all-powerful. But creation reveals little about the heart of God. We need more to go on than what we can see on the surface. We need a deeper look, a divine revelation that will open our hearts and help us to see God in a whole new light. We need both revelation and proclamation. The Lord must somehow speak to us directly… directly and personally. This is where the Word of God comes in. It is through His Word we gain a clearer understanding of what God is like, how He operates, what His purpose is and how He feels about us.

In the passage we now consider, Moses gets more than just a light show. He discovers where all that light emits from. He sees deep into the very heart of the light's source. In short, Moses sees God for who He is and not just how He appears outwardly. As God's brilliance elapses, His name is again proclaimed. Not once, but twice. I imagine Moses had goose bumps from head to toe once He heard the voice echo into the cleft, *"The LORD, The LORD God."* Evidently, this was something Moses was never to forget. We have already touched on the significance of God's name in the previous chapter and discussed it at length in Chapter 20. Now we get some details as to what this name represents and why it is to be revered.

A name is only as good as the one who wears it. It's all about character. While the exact spelling of God's name might be left to conjecture, there is no guesswork concerning His character. That's spelled out very clearly in scripture. And since the history of man, the Lord has proven Himself to be all that He says. Then why must He even say it at all? Is it that we forget? It's not necessarily His character we forget, it's Him we forget. People are kind of dense that way. We need to be reminded of things we already know, important things we tend to stash in the back of our mental file drawer. Sometimes we do this with God, don't we? Other stuff crowds in ahead of Him. He ends up lost in space between our ears. Yet His Word brings Him to the forefront of our minds. Listen carefully to His words to Moses... Let them echo loudly into your thoughts...

The Lord begins by reminding His servant that He is *merciful and gracious*. He is merciful in that He withholds from us what we actually deserve. He is gracious in that He gives us what we don't deserve at all. I think God wanted Moses to remember this for when he returned to camp. This was something which needed to be understood by each and every Israelite. God would withhold His wrath from them though they surely deserved it. He would get them to the promise land, which they didn't deserve at all. Has the Lord not done the same for you and me?

God goes on to say that He is *longsuffering*. Other Bible translations put it this way, "slow to anger." The idea here is that He puts up with a whole lot; He has a very long fuse. Some suppose God to be unusually uptight and hot tempered. They imagine Him perched on the edge of His throne with lightening bolt in hand, ready to chuck it at the first person who steps out of line. They see a severe side of God when they read of the flood or the Sodom and Gomorrah tragedy. But they don't give God credit for putting up with all He did for so long, and how He warned those who would be judged and gave them every opportunity to repent. God doesn't just fly off the handle or blow His stack. He only judges when man gives Him no other option. But listen to His first option:

> *"Come now, and let us reason together, saith the LORD: though your sins be as scarlet, they shall be as white as snow; though they be red like crimson, they shall be as wool"* (Isaiah 1:18).

That's the true heart of God. That's why He puts up with us as much as He does. He truly is longsuffering.

Next, God describes Himself as *abundant in goodness and truth*. What this essentially means is – God is especially kind and exceedingly trustworthy. How many of us can claim the same about ourselves? Few of us might say, I am kind to some people some of the time, but how many of us are kind toward all people all of the time? How many of us can be trusted at all times? *Zilch!* It isn't our nature. Even to have a reputation for being kind or trustworthy we have to work at it. Not God. He's just that way. So long as this is understood, the child of God can rest securely in Him. Never do we need to question our salvation. When we do, it's because we question whether the Lord is truly kind enough to save undeserving sinners. Furthermore, we are questioning the truth of His Word which assures us that He does. If that is you, dear reader, be assured. God is kind.

> *"God is faithful, by whom ye were called unto the fellowship of his Son Jesus Christ our Lord"*
> (1 Corinthians 1:9).

We have covered enough territory to see why the Lord has such a good name among those who believe. But there is still more. The Lord can always be counted on when it comes to *"Keeping mercy for thousands, forgiving iniquity and transgression and sin."* This tells us that God's mercy is continual, it never runs out. He just keeps on forgiving. It matters not what you've done or how many times you've done it, He wipes the slate clean. I like to joke about Santa Claus being legalistic. He makes a list, he checks it twice, he's gonna' find out who's naughty and nice. As the tradition goes, those on the naughty list get a lump of coal. Aren't you glad ol' saint Nick isn't God? Can you imagine if the Lord kept a list? We'd have more than a lump of coal waiting for us! Yet God in His wonderful mercy has made a provision for every sinner to have his slate wiped totally clean. There is no condemnation in Christ Jesus!

As God's glory trailed from sight, Moses was left with this final thought: the Lord would by no means *clear the guilty.* Surely He would visit *the iniquity of the fathers upon the children, and upon the children's children, unto the third and to the fourth generation.* As nice as God is, He is also just. Justice demands that a price be paid for sin. Should one refuse God's payment for sin, then that person must pay for it himself. Sin is passed from one generation to the next. God's Word tells us that each generation will be held accountable. In other words, no one will be able to say, "This is how I was taught." Nor will anyone be able to blame genetics, disease or their environment for their shortcomings. Though that ugly sin nature passes from one generation to the next, each individual must take responsibility for their own actions. But there is hope. The cycle can be broken. We simply accept the payment Jesus made for sin. Only then are the guilty declared innocent.

"The Lord is not slack concerning his promise, as some men count slackness; but is longsuffering to us-ward, not willing that any should perish, but that all should come to repentance" (2 Peter 3:9).

"If we confess our sins, he is faithful and just to forgive us our sins, and to cleanse us from all unrighteousness." 1John 1:9

Section XIII
Exaltation

"The LORD is my strength and song, and he is become my salvation: he is my God, and I will prepare him a habitation; my father's God, and I will exalt him" (Exodus 15:2).

Exalt: [Hebrew, *rum*] to be high, to raise, extol, promote

Revelation and proclamation go hand in hand. God never reveals Himself without proclaiming who He is. The appropriate response on man's part is exaltation. In other words, the Lord is to be lifted up. But what does this actually mean? Can God be lifted any higher? Can little man lift a big God? The answer is – yes! We can lift Him higher in our hearts! Exaltation begins with realization. It is the realization of who God is: that there is none more merciful, more gracious, more longsuffering, kinder, trustworthy or forgiving. There is none holier, righteous or just. Once we realize how great God is we humble ourselves and bow our hearts before Him. The problem with little man is -- we spend too much time thinking about ourselves. We have a tendency to exalt our own interests above all things. Some exalt their many woes above all things. Whether it's self-pride or self-pity, we focus a whole lot on ourselves, don't we? I'm concerned for those who seek to "find themselves." What will happen once they do? Will they celebrate or throw a pity party? Should you desire an honest assessment of who you are, seek God. Once we see Him for all that He is, we begin to understand all that we are. We are not so merciful, gracious, longsuffering, kind, trustworthy or forgiving. We are not so holy, righteous or just. We have but one hope to change all that – God in us! Yes, He is our strength, our song and our salvation. Therefore we prepare a habitation for Him in our hearts. And it is there we exalt Him above all else.

Chapter 27
Going Down in Glory

"So Moses made haste and bowed his head toward the earth, and worshiped" (Exodus 34:8).

Several years ago I was sharing the gospel with English-speaking Africans in a German prison. Most of the inmates who came to hear me were big and intimidating. There was one particular fellow who continued to challenge everything I said. The Lord seemed to give me all the right words to counter his objections, but there was always more to come. Our time together was rapidly running out. The guard announced that I had only one minute left to wrap things up. I finally said to this giant man, "Listen, I gotta go. Do you want to accept Jesus or not?" I practically fell over when he said yes. I led him in a quick prayer then was immediately escorted from the facility. It would be another month before I could return. Naturally, I was quite concerned whether this man's new-found faith would take root and survive in a prison environment. When I returned weeks later, I saw him again. He was beaming from ear to ear. This happy fellow charged right up to me and asked, "What can I do to express my gratitude to God?" The Lord had obviously touched this man. He was an altogether different person. So in awe of God was he, he sought some way to express it.

Likewise, the Lord had revealed Himself in a most profound and personal way to Moses. Even more so than my African friend, Moses was left in complete awe. He sought to express it at once. His response was one of exaltation. Moses immediately went face down and worshipped. I like the fact that he didn't waste any time in doing so. The text tells us, *"So Moses made haste…"* I am reminded of the Christmas story, how it was revealed to those lowly shepherds that Christ was born in a manger. Do you remember their response? The Gospel of Luke states, *"…the shepherds said one to another, Let us now go…"* We then read, *"And they came with haste…"* (Excerpts from Luke 2:15-16.) These anxious fellows couldn't wait to get going. It had been revealed to them where the Christ child could be found and they quickly made a beeline for Him. It was as if they had only one thing on their minds, to be in His presence! The Luke account goes on to say, *"And the shepherds returned, glorifying and praising God for all the things that they had heard and seen, as it was told unto the."* (Luke 2:20).

Each of us would do well to follow the example of these joyful shepherds or the awestruck Moses, who all made haste to exalt their God. While on this topic, I cannot stress enough the importance of morning devotions. Evening devotions are fine, but I think there are greater benefits when we make it our first order of business. Morning devotions seem to shape our dispositions and prepare us for the challenges of life so, why wait? Besides, when we postpone we tend to spend the bulk of our devotional time repenting of things we may have avoided had we met God in the morning! As I mentioned before, it's like when I put on my deodorant. By the end of the day it's too late. Rather than trying to prevent a stench, I'm now trying to cover one up. Now, there is nothing wrong with applying deodorant at night. There's no law that says you can't, and it may even offer some benefit. The same holds true for devotions. But they seem best applied in the morning, and you can always re-apply at night. I also believe morning devotions go along with giving God the first fruits. Because He is worthy of the first fruits, we ought to make haste.

To exalt God is to recognize Him for all that He is. Once we do, we become keenly aware of how insignificant we are. We are outshined by His glory and, at the same time, amazed that a great, big God would place so much worth upon a lowly sinner. This is why Moses went face down and bowed his head toward the earth. Surely he sensed that God's presence was all that mattered. And to be privy to a wonderfully close encounter with the Lord truly humbled Moses. True humility does not mean we dwell on all that is wrong with ourselves. Nor is it something that ushers us into a time of "sacred sulking." True humility means we just don't think of ourselves at all. Yet, the realization that we are in a presence much higher than our own, one we are not worthy of, is very real. And because He accepts us regardless of our wretchedness, our hearts are filled with joy and our lips are filled with praise, adoration and exaltation.

Without a doubt you are familiar with the prayer Jesus taught His apostles to pray. It continues to serve as useful model even today. It is brief, simple yet packed with exaltation. Evidently, Jesus didn't want us to ever lose sight of who we are talking to when we approach our God. Sadly for some, prayer time has become no different than reading off of a wish list to Santa. But you will find nothing self-serving or self-centered in what is commonly referred to as

"The Lord's Prayer,"[1] It is a prayer purely God centered that focuses on His awesomeness. At the very get-go we find the words: *Our Father which art in Heaven.* Here we are reminded that He is high above all things and superior to all creation. The holiness of God is further declared when we say, *"Hallowed be thy name."* Next we are directed toward the will of God, *"Thy kingdom come. Thy will be done in earth, as it is in heaven."* Following these exaltations come the petitions which teach us complete reliance upon One much greater than ourselves. We rely upon His provision and protection. We look to Him as the One who supplies our daily bread and purges the daily leaven from our lives. We even depend upon Him to keep us from temptation as we pray, "deliver us from evil." If you've ever prayed this prayer and missed the awesomeness of God, then you really didn't pray it sincerely. Unfortunately, this holds true for many. This prayer is recited like a well rehearsed script, yet its intent is to fan a flame for God that He might hold an exalted place deep within our hearts.

The Lord had indeed found an exalted place in the heart of His servant Moses. So much so, Moses fell flat on his face and worshipped Him. In this instance the word "worshipped" is translated from the Hebrew term "shachah." It literally means *to fall down flat* or *to do reverence.* This was not a foreign concept in Moses' day. The land of Egypt was filled with people who fell before idols. Then there was the nation of Israel who went face down before a golden calf. It was this very act which caused Moses to seek hard after the Lord. He dared not exalt what the world around him had exalted above the true and living God. This is where we find ourselves today. Exaltation is something which will occur in the heart of every man,

---

[1] Matthew 6:9-13

woman and child. The question is - will you exalt that which the world exalts or will you exalt your God?

A Word After

I'd like to take you back to the question which was proposed at the very onset of this book: What if we really took the daddy of all commandments seriously? What about you, are you ready to get serious with the Lord? Is there a longing in your heart to fall more deeply in love with Him? I sincerely hope that is the case. And I'm hoping you may have picked up a thing or two from our friend, Moses. If there is one thing he learned it is that God blesses those who pursue Him. This isn't just theory, it's a promise:

> *"For he that cometh to God must believe that he is, and that he is a rewarder of them that diligently seek him"* (Hebrews 11:6b).

Please note what the above verse does not say. It does not say, "He is a rewarder of those who seek Him." That would be a welcoming invitation to any who would want to seek God strictly on their own terms. But the text states: "He is a rewarder of them that ***diligently*** seek Him." In other words, we must seek Him whole heartedly. God desires relationship, that's His heart. Once our desire lines up with His, the journey has begun. How about you, do you want what God wants? If the passion is truly there you will take steps similar to those Moses took in his pursuit of God.

For starters, you may want to consider where you have set up camp. Do you find yourself next to the golden calf, or are you within proximity of the Tabernacle of Meeting? Perhaps it is time to pull up stakes and begin your journey, one that will lead you into God's presence. And once you're there, remember, there is always a place closer still! Don't ever let the journey end. As you draw nearer to God, seek to know His way. Always follow His way that you might be a distinguished people, and so others can see God's presence in your life. And never forget, our God is a blessing God. His blessings flood from heaven like a giant waterfall. But you must be standing upon the Rock or you'll miss them. Remain on the Rock. It is there you will enjoy the ultimate view of God's glory!

Printed in the United States
209980BV00001B/70-174/P